THE SUMMER
CAMPAIGN
IN KERRY

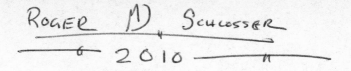

MILITARY HISTORY
OF THE IRISH CIVIL WAR

THE SUMMER CAMPAIGN IN KERRY

TOM DOYLE

SERIES EDITOR: GABRIEL DOHERTY

MERCIER PRESS
IRISH PUBLISHER – IRISH STORY

MERCIER PRESS
Cork
www.mercierpress.ie

Trade enquiries to CMD BookSource,
55a Spruce Avenue, Stillorgan Industrial Park,
Blackrock, County Dublin

© Text: Tom Doyle, 2010

© Foreword: Gabriel Doherty, 2010

ISBN: 978 1 85635 676 3

10 9 8 7 6 5 4 3 2 1

A CIP record for this title is available from the British Library

Printed and bound in the EU.

CONTENTS

Kerry IRA Brigade structure 1919–1923

Acknowledgements

This book would not have been written without the assistance, help and encouragement of many people. I am particularly grateful to Michael Houlihan, Killorglin, whose knowledge of computers proved invaluable at every level in the compilation of this book. Special thanks are also due to Eoin Purcell for his advice and assistance.

I would like to thank many who work in various library services, among them Margaret O'Riordan, branch library, Killorglin; Michael Costello, Local Studies Department, Kerry County Library, Tralee; Mary Sorensen and Kieran Burke, Local Studies Department, Cork City Library; and all who enabled me to consult their vast archive of contemporary newspapers. I would also like to thank Bernadette Gardiner, College Library, NUI Maynooth, Co. Kildare, who enabled me to consult – via an interlibrary loan – Karl Murphy's MA thesis (unpublished) on his grandfather General W.R.E. Murphy's tenure as O/C Kerry, 1922–1923. Special thanks and sincere gratitude to Karl for allowing me to quote from his thesis on General Murphy's involvement in the National Army, Kerry Campaign, August 1922 to January 1923. I would also like to thank Austin Reilly, Killorglin, Co. Kerry, Councillor Patrick O'Connor-Scarteen, Kenmare, Co. Kerry, Patrick J. Lynch, Tarbert, Co. Kerry, and

John Sugrue, Cahirciveen, Co. Kerry, for allowing me to quote excerpts from *The Ohermong Ambush* by Michael Christopher (Dan) O'Shea. Thanks also to Hugh Beckett, Military Archives, Cathal Brugha Barracks, Dublin; Tom Broderick, Ordnance Survey Ireland, and the National Photographic Archive, Temple Bar, Dublin.

Foreword

The role played by Kerry-based IRA units during the War of Independence has at times been a matter of pointed disagreement among students of the Irish struggle for independence, with the balance of recent scholarship tending to the view that these units were more active than conveyed in some earlier accounts. What cannot be denied is that during the Civil War the county witnessed engagements that were as hard-fought as anywhere in the country, as well as some of the most notorious atrocities of the campaign. For a variety of reasons it is these latter actions (which for the most part occurred once the more fluid first stage of the hostilities settled down to the type of guerrilla warfare so familiar from the Anglo-Irish War) that have tended to dominate both public discussion and local popular memory of these terrible months.

Such a focus, however, tells only a part (if a major one) of the totality of the local experience. It certainly diverts attention from the arguably more significant months of July to September 1922, when the scales of war had not yet completely tipped in favour of the National Army, and when Kerry, in the minds of republicans near and far, was seen as much as a bridgehead as a redoubt. As Tom Doyle makes clear in this stimulating work, the balance of military advantage in the region was far from clear-cut during these weeks, with the victory of the forces of the Provisional Government in Limerick (examined in Pádraig Óg Ó Ruairc's volume in this series) being counter-balanced to some extent by the consequent concentration of (numerically strong) republican forces in their 'heartland' areas, their interior lines of communication and the stimulus provided by an awareness of the danger of imminent defeat. It is no exaggeration to say that during this period, culminating in the oft-neglected engagement at Killorglin, history lay in suspended animation. Certainly the leadership on both sides felt so. From the perspective of the Provisional Government this sense that a (or, rather, *the*) moment of crux had arrived was illustrated both by the deployment of ever-larger numbers of troops and by its recourse to emergency powers (legislation being too precise a word to describe parliamentary measures that were, by any standards, of dubious legal merit), while the sense of demoralisation evident amongst republican leaders at the end of September 1922 bore testimony to their realisation that victory had slipped definitively from their grasp.

Behind (or should that be before?) the intentions and actions of military leaders, however, were the fighting men of both sides and the local civilian population. Some of the most stimulating aspects of the book are those that examine how the 'poor bloody infantry', on whose shoulders rested defeat and victory, perceived their station, and (in welcome contrast to so many accounts of military campaigns) the sufferings of the non-combatants caught in the cross-fire (sometimes literally) receive due attention.

It is the balance between the book's treatment of what approximated to 'high' politics and strategy, and its delineation of the experience of those, on both sides and none, who were daily exposed to the horrors of civil war, that is one of its principal merits. It is one that deepens and widens our knowledge of a seminal moment in the modern history of the island of Ireland. I certainly learned a lot from reading it; I believe you will too.

Gabriel Doherty
Department of History
University College Cork

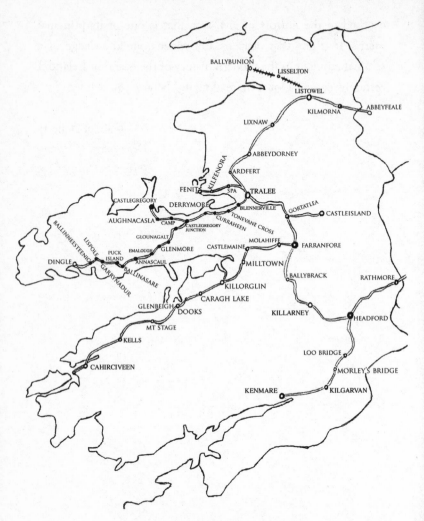

Kerry railway network 1922–1923
During the Civil War, three distinct (private enterprise) railway
companies operated in Kerry:

The Great Southern & Western Railway Company   o=o=o=o
The Tralee to Dingle Railway Company   ●━●━●━●
The Listowel to Ballybunion Railway Company   o⫴⫴⫴o⫴⫴⫴o

INTRODUCTION

In the three weeks between the bombardment of the Four Courts and the shelling of republican strongpoints in Limerick city (28 June–19 July), anti-Treaty forces in both Dublin and Munster took little real action to pre-empt a government military offensive, with the exception of neutralising isolated outposts in Listowel and Skibbereen. In fact they allowed their enemies to determine the early pace and course of the war, despite their vastly superior numbers. At the cessation of hostilities in Dublin, the Provisional Government armed forces numbered little more than 5,000 troops based mostly in the capital. The republicans, on the other hand, had a pool of almost 13,000 volunteers (at least on paper) primarily located in the south and west of the country, who had access to an arsenal of 6,700 rifles.

Politically, Liam Lynch's (IRA Chief-of-Staff) principal objective was to establish the 'Republic' – the ideological 'Holy Grail' – in Munster as a prelude to regaining the initiative nationally. But it is unclear what military policy, or series of strategic military objectives, anti-Treaty forces intended to follow to defeat the government's army on the battlefield. Fundamentally, a republican victory would be a prelude to a resumption of the war against the British. Realistically, had Lynch's forces carried all before them and marched on Dublin, it is probable that the

British army would have intervened (alongside Free State forces) on behalf of the Provisional Government. This scenario was not a prospect that anyone in a position of authority in the Provisional Government wished to consider, except as a last resort.

Viewed from the Provisional Government's GHQ in Dublin, Limerick city was the pivotal strategic military asset in anti-Treaty hands. It had to be neutralised to forestall further military action by the republicans. In early July republicans substantially outnumbered government troops (mainly Michael Brennan's 1st Westerns) based in the city. During July, Brennan and Liam Lynch negotiated a series of truces/ceasefires – a huge tactical blunder on Lynch's part – which bought time for Brennan and allowed Dublin to deploy additional troops, backed up by armoured cars and artillery, to the city. Once they were reinforced, government forces began shelling anti-Treaty fortified positions and three days later, on 21 July 1922, the remaining republicans surrendered. The impact of the defeat nationally was well summed up by Tom McEllistrim, one of the Kerry IRA column commanders engaged in defending the city, who noted: 'Once we failed in Limerick, I knew the war was lost.' Whether McEllistrim's view was widely accepted among republicans in Munster or not, the fighting continued.

Kerry republicans, who were wholeheartedly anti-Treaty, saw the Civil War as a continuation of the War of Independence. In common with the IRA nationally, the Kerry brigades were not consulted by GHQ on the ceasefire or Truce terms. Similarly with the Treaty, they were presented with a *fait accompli*. To add insult to injury there was still considerable resentment of an overhaul GHQ had imposed on the Kerry brigades' leadership during the summer of 1921. Superficially, Kerry republicans saw their refusal to deviate from the 'Republic' proclaimed in 1916 as proof of an ideological purity that had not been compromised by them, unlike the ideals that had been sullied by the plenipotentiaries in London. True, the Kerry republicans may have not deviated an inch, but the ground rules of the society within which the Civil War was taking place had altered beyond recognition from the War of Independence. The War of Independence never threatened Lloyd George's ability to govern Britain, whereas for the Provisional Government a swift military victory was crucial for its political survival. Most Irish people were willing to endure the privations and hardships of 1919–1921 in the expectation of a reasonable political settlement from the British. The general election of 16 June 1922 saw ninety-two TDs returned to the Third Dáil who favoured parliamentary politics (fifty-eight who were pro-Treaty and thirty-four TDs who were ideologically neutral on the Treaty issue) as opposed to thirty-six anti-Treaty TDs, who abstained from participation in the new Dáil. On strictly military terms, GHQ had good intelligence on anti-Treaty forces and their leadership's strengths and weaknesses. As well as this, alongside an overwhelming section of public opinion, the nascent government was also supported by the national press and the Catholic hierarchy.

The decision by the Provisional Government to launch a series of seaborne landings on the Cork and Kerry coast over a ten-day period (2–11 August) was an ambitious and risky strategy. Its success rested on two expectations: firstly, that republicans had prepared for a land-based offensive and had left their sea frontiers undefended, and secondly, that once Cork and Kerry

IRA units based at the 'Front' learned of a Free State invasion, their automatic territorial attachment to their home counties would cause the Limerick/Tipperary front line to implode as the Cork and Kerry contingents returned home to defend their own heartlands. Evidently the military planners in GHQ (Collins, Mulcahy and Dalton) knew their enemy well. Collins' choice to deploy both the Dublin Guards and the 1st Westerns – the most politically reliable and militarily competent forces at his disposal – to Kerry, is proof that he took the Kerry IRA's opposition to his government very seriously.

Almost overnight, and without warning, 940 government troops gained a foothold at opposite ends of the county (Tarbert and Kenmare) and occupied the county town of Tralee, sustaining relatively few casualties. On 12 August, two days after the fall of Cork city, Collins was confident enough of his own position to personally visit Tralee with the aim of opening preparatory discussions with the republican leadership and negotiating an end to the war in Kerry. However, while in Tralee he learned of the death of his government colleague, Arthur Griffith. He cut short his visit, aborted the discussions agenda and returned to Dublin. Leaving Tralee, Collins probably felt he was witnessing the beginning of the end of republican resistance in Kerry. But to quote Winston Churchill on another conflict: 'It was not the beginning of the end, rather, it was the end of the beginning.'

While the pro-Treaty force deployed to establish a secure foothold in Kerry had been sufficient to establish a beachhead, as it spread itself further and further across the county, its effect as a military force diminished. Perhaps half the initial landing of 940 troops was tied down to static positions by late August, in effect making pro-Treaty forces deployed in Kerry largely defensive in nature. By this time the republicans had virtually shut down Kerry's rail network, forcing all military and civilian traffic onto the roads. Furthermore, virtually all the troops deployed in the county were from outside Kerry – with the exception of the Kenmare garrison – and the lack of local knowledge further stymied the force's effectiveness. An additional 500–1,000 men would have tilted the balance in the Free State army's favour, counteracting in some ways the natural advantages the Kerry IRA units possessed over their adversaries.

While the republicans could choose to ignore the political considerations that underpinned the conflict, the IRA in Kerry could not ignore the military realities that they had to deal with. Virtually overnight, the Provisional Government had been able to land 940 troops in Kerry and establish military control as a prelude to establishing 'civil' power and political authority over the county. Territory held by the republicans had been lost and both forces would now have to fight it out for control of the county. However, while the pro-Treaty forces had the initial success, within a week of the landings the IRA in Kerry had begun to recover their nerve. By early September – with prompting from Liam Deasy's 1st Southern Division – Kerry IRA units were developing a co-ordinated strategy to attack all the military outposts in a town as a way of overwhelming the garrison. This strategy was to reach its zenith with the assault on Killorglin at the end of September 1922. It was the failure to achieve their objective in Killorglin on 27 September that marked a turning point in the IRA campaign in Kerry. From then on operations on this scale were never again attempted in the county. However, the passing of the Emergency

Powers Act in the Dáil on the same day also acknowledged that after three months in the field, the efforts of the Provisional Government's army on its own were not sufficient to defeat the republicans.

CHAPTER 1

FROM THE TREATY VOTE TO THE KERRY LANDINGS

On 7 January 1922, the Dáil endorsed the terms of the Treaty by sixty-four votes to fifty-seven, a pro-Treaty majority of seven. In a mature democracy that would have settled the issue – a majority vote in the Irish Assembly should have been accepted by the defeated faction. But many of the deputies returned in the May 1921 election came from the physical force tradition rather than a heritage imbued in constitutional and parliamentary procedures. As they viewed it, national independence had been won (and the Republic proclaimed in 1916 could still be achieved) by the IRA bullet rather than by a popular ballot.

During the vote on the Treaty, all members of the Dáil were entitled to outline their reasons for why they voted the way they did. The Kerry/West Limerick constituency had returned eight TDs (unopposed) on the Sinn Féin ticket in the 1921 general election, but only two of these TDs, Austin Stack and Fionán Lynch, representing opposite sides of the argument, elaborated and explained their positions. Austin Stack alluded to his Fenian heritage and the fact that his father had served time in an English jail for his republican ideals as reason enough to reject the Treaty. He also personalised his stance as one of loyalty to Éamon de Valera. Fionán Lynch approved the Treaty because it gave Ireland its own army, enabled the British army to withdraw from Ireland and gave the state control over its own financial and educational systems. The fact that Michael Collins was willing to accept the Treaty was sufficient reason to support it, Lynch argued. The remaining Kerry TDs did not contribute to the debate, but Thomas O'Donoghue and Paddy J. Cahill joined Austin Stack in the 'No' lobby, while Piaras Béaslaí and James Crowley voted in favour.

As a result of the pro-Treaty majority, de Valera resigned as president of the Dáil. On 10 January the Assembly reconvened to elect a new leader. De Valera ran as a candidate in an attempt to regain control of the Dáil agenda. However, Arthur Griffith won the vote, securing sixty votes to de Valera's fifty-eight, whereupon de Valera and his supporters left the Dáil. On 14 January, the sixty pro-Treaty TDs and the four Unionist MPs returned by Dublin University (Trinity) formed a Provisional Government that would hold the reins of power until a 'Free State' (based on parliamentary elections) could be established.

Following Cathal Brugha's resignation as Defence Minister on 10 January, Richard Mulcahy assumed responsibility for the IRA and its relationship with both the Dáil and the Provisional Government. The next day, 11 January, IRA leaders such as Rory O'Connor, Liam Mellows, Oscar Traynor and Liam Lynch met and demanded that Mulcahy should hold a Volunteer Convention on 5 February, to ascertain the army's position on the Treaty. This demand sent the Provisional Government a mixed message: on the one hand it gave Mulcahy de facto recognition as a government representative, but on the other proclaimed that the IRA's loyalty to the Provisional Government (and the terms it accepted from the British) could not be taken for granted. Mulcahy managed to secure an extension of one month on the army convention. This 11 January meeting papered over the cracks in the IRA, preserving the myth of army unity, an essential prerequisite for the British withdrawal. From this point onwards, British military and police forces began to evacuate their barracks and other installations, and hand them over to local IRA units. They began evacuating the smaller and more remote areas of the country first, in the process giving anti-Treaty forces control of substantial parts of the country. Within a few weeks all the major towns in Kerry and their military installations were under republican control. For Collins this British military withdrawal was crucial, and – in the short term at least – more important than surrendering local control to his anti-Treaty adversaries. He was worried that anti-Treaty groups would attack crown forces as a way of reopening hostilities in the Anglo-Irish War.

Griffith argued that it would be to the government's advantage to hold an election on the Treaty issue sooner rather than later, but Collins postponed a decision on the electoral front. In the spring of 1922 it was more important to him to preserve Sinn Féin and IRA 'unity' than obtain a popular mandate for the Treaty and the Provisional/Free State Government. The Provisional Government didn't yet have an army to confront (nor did they want to challenge) their former comrades. So, by postponing a decision on the election, the new government could consolidate its position, and in so doing attempt to win over more people in the anti-Treaty camp to at least a 'neutral' position (i.e. opposed to the Treaty, but not willing to take up arms against the government). To do so was essential to the Provisional Government's chances of survival, as many of the most experienced IRA members were initially staunchly anti-Treaty.

Even before the Dáil had voted on the issue in January, in Kerry all the brigade commanders had declared to the men under their jurisdiction that they would not support or argue for acceptance of the terms of the Treaty. To an extent their statement was a declaration of solidarity with the line taken by Austin Stack. In practical terms, Florence O'Donoghue, from Rathmore, and Deputy Leader of the IRA's 1st Southern Division, estimated that during the War of Independence the Kerry IRA at full strength could draw from a pool of 8,750 Volunteers from their three brigade areas, broken down as follows:

Kerry No. 1 Brigade	4,000
Kerry No. 2 Brigade	3,400
Kerry No. 3 Brigade	1,350[1]

Effectively about 1,000 of the Kerry IRA would take up arms against the Provisional Government and work to undermine and overthrow the regime it was imposing on Kerry and Ireland.

On 1 February 1922, the first unit of the Provisional Government's army, resplendent in their new uniforms, marched past City Hall (where Collins took the salute) en route to Beggar's Bush barracks, the National Army's new headquarters. It was made up of forty-six men drawn mainly from the Dublin Brigade, under the command of thirty-two-year-old Captain Paddy O'Daly, a veteran of the 1916 Rising and O/C of Collins' 'Squad' during the War of Independence. This unit would grow and evolve into the Dublin Guards Regiment, which by the outbreak of hostilities in June/July would consist of two battalions (900–1,000 men) under Brigadier General O'Daly. Apart from the members of the 'Squad' (with its culture of assassination and personal loyalty to Collins), the new regiment also had a substantial number of pro-Treaty members of the Northern Division of the IRA (Donegal, Monaghan and Belfast) among its officers and other ranks, as well as raw recruits, predominantly Dubliners, who saw the army as a refuge from unemployment.

In Kerry, during the same month, a different army was making preparations for the conflict ahead, with a raid that was – superficially at least – the Civil War equivalent of the Gortlea raid of 1918. At 9 p.m. on Saturday 11 February, thirty armed men marched on Castleisland barracks, which was still occupied by twelve RIC constables. Locking the policemen in the guardroom, they took rifles, revolvers, arms, ammunition and grenades.[2] It is almost certain that Tom McEllistrim's column carried out the raid to make provision for what they believed was the inevitable confrontation when the Provisional Government tried to impose its writ on Kerry.

On 18 February, Commander Thomas Malone of the Mid Limerick Division publicly declared for the Republic, and repudiated GHQ's claim to speak for the IRA. The move had serious implications for the government's two provincial enclaves, Michael Brennan's 1st Westerns in Clare and Seán McEoin's forces in Athlone, both of which could potentially be isolated and overwhelmed by concerted attacks by anti-Treaty forces. A week later, Ernie O'Malley, Commander of the 2nd Southern Division (which included Malone's Mid Limerick Brigade), raided Clonmel police depot. The republican units acquired 293 rifles, 273 revolvers, 3 Lewis (machine) guns and 324,000 rounds of ammunition, as well as 11 motor cars, making the 2nd Southern Division one of the best-equipped autonomous military groups in the country.[3] It gave O'Malley huge leverage and he threw down the gauntlet to the Dublin Brigade and the 1st Westerns that GHQ had sent to Limerick to buttress up the small pro-government garrison, calling on them to leave the city. During a stand-off in late February and early March both sides brought in reinforcements, bringing both groups up to parity, with about 700 men on each side. On 10 March 1922, GHQ seized the initiative and Mulcahy summoned Liam Lynch and Oscar Traynor to Beggar's Bush barracks (Dublin) to diffuse the situation. They persuaded O'Malley to back down. The resolution was a diplomatic 'victory' for Mulcahy, who learned a lot more from the experience than his anti-Treaty rivals.

Following what was in effect a regional coup attempt, Mulcahy took measures to give the Provisional Government a military presence in Munster, setting up garrisons at Skibbereen and Listowel in late February–early March. The Listowel unit consisted of about 250 men, mostly raw recruits, with NCOs and officers drawn from the War of Independence veterans who had declared themselves pro-Treaty at the start of the year. Under the command of Thomas J. Kennelly, who had led the North Kerry flying column during the War of Independence, the Kerry Brigade was billeted in Listowel workhouse. It was a well-equipped force, having received 200 rifles, 4 Lewis guns, large quantities of ammunition, new uniforms and a Crossley Tender (lorry) from GHQ on 3 March 1922.[4] However, by late March 1922, anti-Treaty manpower and weaponry in the south and west of the country numbered 12,900 troops, who had an arsenal of 6,780 rifles.

On 15 March, Mulcahy cancelled the 'Army Convention' which was due to take place in Dublin on 26 March. In tandem with this, all GHQ financing of the brigades and divisions unwilling to acknowledge its authority was suspended. On 22 March, Rory O'Connor held a press conference where he proclaimed that he represented over 80 per cent of the IRA and that in ignoring the wishes of the majority of the members, GHQ was smothering the democratic wishes of the IRA. Ignoring Mulcahy's orders, a total of 223 delegates attended the Dublin meeting, which was not attended by any GHQ representatives, with members from fifty-two out of the seventy-three War of Independence brigades attending. The 1st and 2nd Southern Divisions sent fifty-four and twenty-eight delegates respectively, while the four Western Divisions had sixty-nine representatives. O'Connor would claim the allegiance of twelve of the country's sixteen IRA divisions.

The convention elected a sixteen-member executive, on which O'Connor, Liam Mellows and Ernie O'Malley were the principal spokesmen. The *Freeman's Journal* published a highly critical editorial, focusing on O'Connor's comments about the possibility of setting up a military dictatorship. Press freedom was clearly not a priority for the executive and on the night of 29 March, the IRA burned down the newspaper's Dublin headquarters. The phoenix that would rise from the ashes would become a fierce critic of the anti-Treaty military campaign and one of the most trenchant supporters of the government's repressive measures adopted against the republicans.

In a highly symbolic gesture, members of Dublin No. 1 Brigade seized the Four Courts on the night of 13–14 April (Holy Thursday–Good Friday) in a move that reclaimed the mantle of the 1916 Rebellion and threw down the gauntlet to the Provisional Government. Liam Mellows, secretary of the executive, read out the group's demands. No elections could be held while British occupation of the country continued. The Civic Guards should be disbanded, and any further recruitment into the Provisional Government's army should cease. The Dáil should reinstate and continue to pay all the executive's financial and operating expenses. While high on symbolism, this emotionally charged act was unaccompanied by any coherent military strategy. The 200 men in the garrison, for instance, made no attempt to fortify the vast complex of buildings at any point between the initial seizure and the eventual government assault almost two and a half months later.

Michael Collins was due to address two pro-Treaty rallies in Killarney and Tralee over the weekend of 22–23 April 1922. Notices were put up in and around Killarney by Kerry No. 2 Brigade, IRA, proscribing the rally and advising those attending that republicans could not guarantee their safety if they attended. The platform erected for the meeting was burnt to the ground. When Collins and his entourage, Kevin O'Higgins, Seán McEoin and Fionán Lynch and a twelve-man security detail under Joe Dolan's command, arrived on the platform of Killarney railway station on Saturday, they were met by a heavily armed anti-Treaty force. The confrontation was defused by the intervention of the local Franciscan abbot, who offered the Friary grounds as a venue for Collins' speech. Providing Collins with a brake (trailer) as a platform, the meeting went ahead, though with a much reduced attendance.

Tralee republicans surpassed their Killarney counterparts in their efforts to undermine the staging of a pro-Treaty meeting in their town. Special trains laid on to transport government supporters from Kenmare, Killarney, and Newcastle West were unable to travel because sections of the line had been taken up – only the 'Special' from Dingle reached Tralee. The gates on railway level crossings were opened across the road and chained shut, making an effective barricade for all road traffic. Following the Killarney stand-off, it was deemed necessary to reinforce Joe Dolan's force, and a further twenty-four men under the control of Denny Galvin of Knocknagoshel were drafted in to provide assistance. However, as with Killarney, after a stand-off in Tralee, Collins was able to deliver his planned address there. This convinced him that while Kerry republicans could talk a hard fight, their actions would not speak as loud as their words and that if he had cause to send troops to Kerry at a later date, any military stand-off might be relatively short-lived.

This theory would soon be tested when, on 1 May 1922, 150 troops drawn from Kerry No. 1 and Kerry No. 2 Brigades marched on Listowel and set up a cordon of outposts around the Provisional Government's military headquarters in the town. This led to a two-month-long stand-off between the Provisional Government garrison and republicans in Listowel, which came to a violent end with the outbreak of hostilities in Dublin on 28 June. On Friday 30 June, at 8.30 a.m., republicans opened fire on Free State troops billeted in J.J. Walsh's drapery shop on

Market Street, while soldiers based in the Listowel Arms Hotel on the square came under fire from anti-Treaty forces based in R.M. Danagher's shop on the opposite side of the square. Private Patrick Sheehy, a twenty-year-old serving with the government force whose father was an insurance broker in the town, was killed, while Lieutenant Donalin O'Grady of the Free State army was wounded.[5]

Tom Kennelly, the Free State commander, was anxious to bring the conflict to a quick end and avoid any further loss of life on either side. Fr Charles Troy, a native of Listowel, then a post-graduate student from Dunboyne, County Meath, studying in Maynooth though serving in the Dublin Archdiocese, put himself forward as an intermediary and successfully brokered a ceasefire.[6] At 5 p.m. that same evening, the Free State garrison surrendered to the republicans. Tom Kennelly, O/C Listowel garrison, and Humphrey Murphy, O/C Kerry No. 1 Brigade, issued a joint statement to the effect that as Kerrymen neither side wanted to fight each other in a civil war.

The *Republican Bulletin*, quoted in the *Cork Examiner*, reported that the republican forces at Listowel captured an armoured car, two Lewis guns, 150 rifles and several private cars. Fifty members of the captured garrison threw in their lot with the republicans, opting to join with them and go to the front in Limerick. The remaining 200 prisoners were transferred to Ballymullen barracks in Tralee.[7] Republicans in west Cork took comparable action to the Kerry brigades, launching an attack on the Free State garrison in Skibbereen early in July. In the process they neutralised Mulcahy's second outpost in Munster. The *Republican Bulletin's* account of events in Listowel was accurate, except for the fact that the garrison didn't have an armoured car, a piece of equipment far too rare and valuable to assign to a provincial outpost in early March, when the Listowel garrison was first established. The British only began supplying armoured vehicles and artillery in critical numbers to the Provisional Government when hostilities commenced in Dublin. This information was included exclusively for propaganda purposes aimed at a civilian audience, as the military authorities in Dublin knew the Listowel garrison didn't have an armoured car. However, the loss of 20 per cent of the garrison (fifty men) who defected to the republican side on surrender was true and an extremely worrying precedent for the government. An army that could not depend either politically or militarily on its own troops in a conflict had a major problem.

After the fall of the Four Courts in Dublin on 30 June, Liam Lynch and Liam Deasy, the two senior commanders of the 1st Southern Division who were attending an executive army convention meeting in the capital, were allowed (with Mulcahy's approval) to return to Munster, where both Collins and Mulcahy anticipated they would be a moderating influence and do their utmost to avoid continuing the conflict. The government miscalculated in this assessment; as far as Lynch was concerned the die was cast when Collins ordered his troops to shell the Four Courts, thereby commencing (if not actually declaring) war on not just the executive headquarters, but on the entire republican/anti-Treaty military organisation. Lynch now took charge of a substantial second front in Munster from which the republicans intended to launch a major counter-attack against the Free State forces. On paper the front line stretched from Limerick city to Waterford city.

In Kerry the republicans were preparing for the coming conflict with the Provisional Government's forces. On Monday 11 July 1921 – the day the Truce was declared – five republicans had been killed in Castleisland (three British troops were also killed) in what was, by pure coincidence, the last military action of the War of Independence, not only in Kerry but also at national level. The commemoration of the first anniversary of this event was turned into a major political rally. According to the *Cork Examiner*:

Captain Richard Shanahan, Lieutenant John Flynn and NCO John Prendeville led the procession to Castleisland cemetery, which was reviewed by Diarmuid O'Leary O/C and attended by over 1,000 Volunteers, Cumann na mBan and Fianna Éireann who marched in military formation to the republican plot. Rev Fr Myles Allman, CC, addressed the gathering: 'They [the men killed in the Castleisland ambush] believed in the argument of physical force and went light-heartedly into battle against a superior number of forces. Today, being laid to rest is the former Minister of Defence, Cathal Brugha, his body riddled with bullets of an alien enemy. Acceptance of a Treaty and a Constitution will ensure that Irishmen will deprive Irishmen of their place among the nations of the world.'[8]

Father Allman was from a staunchly republican family and his brother Dan was killed during the Headford ambush in March 1921. He had no doubts about the continuity between the War of Independence and the Civil War, and the path that the Kerry IRA would have to follow to achieve the Republic proclaimed in 1916.

A similar, though a much smaller, commemoration was held at Rath Cemetery in Tralee. The two orations at these commemorations were used to motivate the troops, as various IRA units in Kerry were already preparing to send contingents to the front in Limerick city and county. Patrick Foran (20) of Lisselton, County Kerry, was among the wounded in Limerick city. He subsequently died of his injuries on 26 July thereby becoming the first Kerry republican killed in the Civil War.[9]

Following the fall of Limerick city, evacuating republican forces converged on their existing strongpoint based around Bruree, Bruff and Kilmallock in east Limerick, where the major road and rail links between Dublin, Cork and Limerick cities converged. The front line in east Limerick was the nearest the Civil War came to conventional warfare, and as such favoured the support structures of a conventionally organised army rather than a force like the War of Independence IRA, who operated what might be described as a 'hit and run' policy. Surprise and the ability to inflict a lot of injuries on lots of men in a short period of time was the core of their military experience, skills not really suited to the conduct of conventional warfare. Kerry units were active in the fighting in east Limerick. Charles Hanlon of Listowel was wounded in Bruree on 26 July and died of his wounds on 4 August 1922.[10]

Already by this point public opinion in Kerry was beginning to focus on the worrying speed at which major hostilities had catapulted from Dublin a month earlier and were now in their own backyard. On the evening of Monday 24 July, the Kerry Farmers' Union organised a public meeting at Tralee Court House. Representatives of the labour movement and commercial interests were also present at the meeting, which was presided over by Mr John T. O'Neill, President of the Kerry Farmers' Union, who called on members of Dáil Éireann for Kerry/West Limerick to press for the immediate summoning of the Dáil to hold a meeting to bring about peace. Humphrey Murphy, O/C Kerry No. 1 Brigade, also addressed the meeting, outlining events as he saw them evolving if the government chose to continue a policy of war:

> If the Provisional Government continue to fight with English guns, English bullets and shells, English armoured cars and the ex-soldiers of the English army … I am certain they are going to fail as the Black and Tans failed, because the war did not come properly until it comes to Cork and Kerry. We will defend every town to the last. You will have towns in ruins and famine finishing those who have escaped the bullet. We will stop at nothing, and we are going to win even if it takes years.[11]

Murphy's blood-curdling rhetoric must have made the hair stand up on the back of the necks of the audience, who listened to the twenty-eight-year-old former teacher from Currow elaborate on the fate he had in store for both the army of the newly elected government and, by default, the civilian population of Kerry once hostilities began in the county. Of course it is important to realise that Murphy's comments weren't delivered just for the benefit of his immediate audience. He was also speaking in the aftermath of the fall of Limerick, a major military set-back for the republican cause in Munster. And in this context he needed to boost both the morale of his own troops and issue a warning to his adversaries, still drunk on the euphoria of victory.

Chapter 2

The Quays of the Kingdom

It was Emmett Dalton who suggested a series of seaborne landings on the Cork and Kerry coasts as a way of foreshortening and undermining the military cohesion of the Munster Republic.[1] Born in Dublin in 1897, Dalton was from a Redmondite family and joined the Royal Dublin Fusiliers in 1914 as a private, aged seventeen. Showing a good deal of initiative, he was soon promoted to corporal. During action in the First World War he rallied his men when their officer was killed and successfully repelled an attack by a more numerous German force, which earned him a commission. He was awarded the Military Medal on the Somme. By the end of the Great War Dalton had attained the rank of major, serving as the aide-de-camp for Field Marshal Sir Henry Wilson, whose assassination in June 1922 precipitated the attack on the Four Courts that started the Civil War.

Emmett Dalton's younger brother, Charlie, who was in the Dublin Brigade (IRA), facilitated his introduction to Michael Collins after the First World War. Collins valued his military expertise not only for its own sake, but also because of the invaluable insights Dalton provided into the mindset of the upper echelon 'Top Brass' that constituted the core of the Chief Imperial General Staff. During the Treaty negotiations in London, Dalton played a central role in organising the Irish delegation's security measures, including having an aeroplane on stand-by in case the team had to leave London at short notice if the talks failed. In the early months of 1922, Dalton, aided by J.J. 'Ginger' O'Connell, who had served in the American army, tried to train a professional Irish army. This proved to be a difficult task as none of the IRA who stayed with the pro-Treaty army had much in the way of conventional military skills or training. In common with their anti-Treaty adversaries, most of their War of Independence experiences were engagements that were opportunistic, or sporadic attacks and ambushes that took place at a local level and on a small scale without any sense of a wider tactical or strategic pattern or template.

Dalton's First World War experience and his arguments for the landings were compelling. If government troops landed behind enemy lines, the Cork and Kerry contingents – some of the most experienced and battle-hardened troops on the anti-Treaty side – would be forced to abandon the front line in favour of returning home to defend their own areas. Not only would the Limerick–Waterford line collapse, but avoiding costly and protracted rearguard actions by republicans at every crossroads and hillock across west Limerick, north Cork and east Kerry would save the lives of scores of government troops. Michael Collins and Richard Mulcahy gave Dalton's proposal full support.

On the ground and at sea it was the job of brigade commanders to translate strategic objectives into practical working solutions. The men who would be responsible for this action were General Eoin O'Duffy and General W.R.E. Murphy. O'Duffy was in charge of the South Western Division, which included north Kerry, north Cork, Limerick and Clare, and parts of south Galway and north Tipperary, with Murphy, a veteran of the First World War, serving as his adjutant. O'Duffy's experience as an IRA commander during the War of Independence, combined with Murphy's experience as a commander of conventional military forces, was seen as an ideal command combination.[2] O'Duffy was over-confident and underestimated the resolve of the Kerry IRA to face the challenge of the Provisional Government. O'Duffy's view of the Kerry IRA's performance during the War of Independence was equally dismissive and ludicrous: 'Kerry's entire record in the Black and Tan struggle consisted in the shooting of an unfortunate soldier on the day of the Truce.'[3]

THE LANDING AT FENIT

We are fortunate to have an excellent first-hand account of the preparation and execution of the Free State army's task force that landed in Fenit in early August 1922. Niall Harrington, a twenty-one-year-old trainee pharmacist from Dublin, joined the Army Medical Service (AMS), as a medical assistant with the rank of corporal, and was seconded to the Dublin Guards, the unit to which Collins had assigned the task of establishing a government military enclave in Kerry. From a distinguished Home Rule/Redmondite family, Harrington was no stranger to Kerry. His father, Timothy, first elected MP for Dublin in the Parnellite landslide election of 1885 and later lord mayor of

Dublin, was, along with his brother Edward (an MP for Kerry), one of the chief architects of the Irish Parliamentary Party 'Plan of Campaign' during the Land War. Another brother, Dan, was the owner/editor of *The Kerry Sentinel*, which supported the Land League/Home Rule position in Kerry between 1879–1913. Following his father's death in 1910, Niall Harrington made several visits to Tralee, where his uncle Dan lived until his death in 1913, and was more familiar with Tralee and its surroundings than most of the others on board the *Lady Wicklow*.

The Provisional Government chartered this 262-foot vessel to serve as troop transport to bring a task force of 450 men, four companies of the Dublin Guards, to Fenit. The ship's Master, John Theodore Rogers, was not at all happy to have his vessel requisitioned for military purposes, given the fate of the *Aud*, the boat used by the Irish Volunteers six years earlier in April 1916 in an attempt to offload German arms in Tralee Bay. On that occasion the ship had been intercepted by the Royal Navy and the commander ended up having to scuttle his ship along with its contents – arms and ammunition. Rogers would have been well aware of the possibility of his ship coming under hostile fire, if not actual destruction, as it approached the Kerry coast.

Arriving at the ship's embarkation point at 10.30 p.m. on Monday 31 July, Harrington learned that the departure was delayed, as they were awaiting the arrival of eighty additional troops. In addition to its complement of men, the cargo included an 18-pounder field gun, which the troops would later nickname 'The Rose of Tralee', and a Rolls-Royce Whippet armoured car with a rotating tower and Vickers machine-guns. It was the first armoured car that the army had received from the British and was nicknamed 'Ex Mutineer', as it had been commandeered by republicans at the time of the assault on the Four Courts, but was recaptured during the course of the Free State victory.[4] In spite of this complement of armour and artillery, it was still the ordinary soldier with his rifle who would bear the brunt of the campaign against the republicans in Kerry. However, the advantage of having these additional weapons gave the Free State army the upper hand in many encounters with republicans during the course of the war and saved the lives of many government troops in Kerry.

Brigadier Paddy O'Daly, O/C of the Dublin Guards, had the ultimate responsibility for the delivery of a successful landing, and was assisted by Commandant James Dempsey and Vice Commandant James McGuinness. An indication of the serious-ness Collins placed on a swift, successful campaign in Kerry was the inclusion of two of his most effective intelligence officers from the War of Independence days, James McNamara and David Neligan. Their role was to collect information on the strength and disposition of the IRA. And yet O'Daly, in tandem with both Collins and Mulcahy, seriously underestimated the contribution that Kerry republicans had made during the campaign against the British in 1919–1921. Collins in particular felt that once the Kerry IRA put up a 'token' resistance to the Provisional Government's forces, its campaign would wind down after a few weeks and it would agree to negotiate an end to the conflict.

Leaving Dublin at midday on Tuesday 1 August, the *Lady Wicklow* approached the Kerry coast at first light the next day. Niall Harrington was roused from his sleep by Commandant David Neligan with the news that the force's senior commander, Paddy O'Daly, wanted to talk to him. O'Daly was alone in his cabin and was poring over some maps of Tralee and its hinterland. He asked Harrington's opinion on the various routes he might use to capture Ballymullen barracks and other key military installations. Interestingly, the young corporal's innovative suggestion, that he delay the landing until after dark and thereby take the objectives and their garrisons in a surprise attack, was overruled by O'Daly, who explained that he was under orders to capture Tralee by 12.30 p.m. that day.

The plan of attack, as outlined by Harrington, was that the troops would land in Fenit and advance to Spa, where the force would split and form a pincer movement. A column under Captain Billy McClean would advance along Strand Road, encircling the town via Blennerville and Ballyard, and hopefully neutralise any republican resistance it met on its way. Meanwhile, the main body of the army would enter Tralee at Pembroke Street, where some of the men, under Dempsey's command, would advance along the railway line and head for the workhouse and Ballymullen barracks, while the remaining troops under O'Daly and McGuinness would progress via Rock Street and rejoin McClean's column in the square/Bridge Street. At this point, assuming everything had gone according to plan, they would advance towards Moyderwell Cross, capture the 'Staff' barracks, reunite with Dempsey's column and surround and take Ballymullen barracks.[5]

Though he didn't know it at the time of the invasion, Harrington would later learn that O'Daly had no intelligence on either the strength, disposition or the defences of the republican forces he would encounter as the troops under his command set foot on Kerry soil. Apart from the fact that he knew that all the three Kerry brigades were staunchly anti-Treaty, he wasn't aware that many of the 'flower' of those same brigades, possibly as many as 250–300 of Kerry's most experienced fighting men, were in service on the front line of the 'Munster Republic', principally in east Limerick. When Niall Harrington suggested an invasion under the cover of darkness, he didn't realise the irony that the daylight attack was taking place almost totally in the dark.

When Napoleon was told of an officer who would make a good commander he asked: 'Yes, but is he lucky?' This quip was very apt in the case of the Fenit landing. O'Daly and the men under his command were very lucky. The expedition didn't have any form of bridging equipment as a contingency if circumstances at Fenit prevented an actual landing at the pier. Amazingly, there was no qualified doctor accompanying the Dublin Guards to Kerry; the most senior medical orderly on board was Sergeant Ted Keating from Dundalk, County Louth. Given the numbers of men who served in the Dublin Fusiliers during the First World War it is inconceivable that there were no military surgeons who could have been recruited to accompany the Dublin Guards expedition.

The defensive measures that awaited O'Daly's force at Fenit were mainly the result of the suspicions of Paddy Cahill, Commander of the 9th Battalion, that the Free State might land troops in Kerry. If they did so, he believed that Fenit, Tarbert and (possibly) Dingle would be the most likely landing areas. Cahill had been demoted from O/C of Kerry No. 1 Brigade following GHQs restructuring of the Kerry IRA during the summer of 1921. His leadership during the War of Independence was seen as too conservative and not aggressive enough in challenging the British. Following his demotion he was given command of the

9th Battalion, a unit created by Kerry IRA colleagues as a face-saving exercise. If his precautionary measures had been heeded and properly implemented, especially in Tralee, the republicans would have posed a serious challenge to the Dublin Guards, both at the initial landing at Fenit and later at the approaches to Tralee town. Cahill asked John Joe Sheehy, senior officer of Tralee IRA, to draw up a defensive plan both for Fenit pier and the north-western approaches to Tralee town which was passed on to Humphrey Murphy, O/C Kerry No. 1 Brigade. Murphy approved the Cahill/Sheehy plan and on 15 July a small garrison of twenty men drawn from the 1st Battalion (Tralee) and the 7th Battalion (Castleisland) under Tony Sheehy and Seamus O'Connor were installed at the coastguard station at Fenit, which gave them an unrivalled view of the 250-foot stone pier and the 700-foot wooden causeway that joined it to the mainland. A landmine strategically located at the centre of the causeway served as the lynchpin of the defences. Theoretically it would be detonated on the arrival of a suspicious vessel and the invading force would be isolated on the pier, allowing the garrison to pin down the government troops until their own reinforcements arrived.

The arrival of the coastguard 'garrison' was viewed with a mixture of suspicion and foreboding by many of the fishermen and Harbour Commissioner staff working out of Fenit. They quickly realised the landmine's potential to destroy the port and in the process their livelihoods, leaving them without work long after both belligerents had left the area. As time passed, the more observant noticed that the garrison did not examine the landmine on anything like a regular basis. On Thursday 27 July at 4 a.m., two employees of the Harbour Commissioners, acting without any political motivation other than to preserve their jobs, disconnected the cable attaching the explosives to the detonator.[6]

For the defence of Tralee town, Sheehy had recommended placing sniper units in Latchford's Mills, a four-storey warehouse on Nelson (Ashe) Street, where their field of fire would cover Nelson Street, Castle Street and the Great Southern & Western Railway station. An additional small force located in the GS&WR's goods depot on Edward Street would widen the scope to cover the Dingle railway station and yards, and the 'New Line'. If these posts had been manned, the entire area could have become a lethal killing ground for many of the government troops as they entered Tralee.

Shortly before 10 a.m. on the morning of Wednesday 2 August, the *Lady Wicklow* approached Fenit. As there was no prior notification of any vessel docking that morning, and as the tide was unsuitable for an immediate landing, John Fitzgerald, the harbour pilot, got his two sons to row him out to the mystery vessel. As soon as he was on board he noticed the armoured car under the tarpaulin, but as his sons were already on their way back to shore he had little option but to assist the berthing of the ship, which proved difficult because of the tidal conditions. Sergeant Jack Lydon, a senior NCO with the Dublin Guards (aged twenty-eight), from James' Street, Tralee, provided invaluable assistance and so the *Lady Wicklow* was successfully berthed at Fenit Pier at 10.30 a.m. From his vantage point on shore, almost 700 yards away, Johnny Sheehan, a republican sentry, could make out uniformed men on the deck of the ship that had just docked. He rushed off to alert the garrison and warn the locals that a landing was imminent.

As soon as the commander got word, he detonated the switch to activate the landmine, but nothing happened. Repeated attempts proved equally futile. Meanwhile some of the troops were already descending onto the pier, on which a long line of railway wagons stretching the length of the causeway provided fortuitous cover. Nevertheless a number of defenders on the republican side fired at the ship, managing to wound some of the soldiers as they descended the gangplank. Immediately following this the armoured car, still strapped to the deck of the *Lady Wicklow*, opened up with a massive volley of machine-gun fire. It would have been suicidal for any of the garrison to even attempt resistance. Republican Tom Flynn was killed on the beach near Fenit. Interestingly, the *Republican Bulletin* – a mixture of fact, misinformation and downright propaganda that was edited by Frank Gallagher and published daily in the *Cork Examiner* while the republicans still held the city (Cork fell on 11 August) – recorded that a British navy sloop bombarded Fenit, successfully assisting the Free State landing.[7]

Unfortunately for the republicans they were unable to inform their other units beyond Fenit of the landing, because Mrs Kelly, the local post-mistress and telephone exchange operator, became hysterical once the shooting began and was too preoccupied with saying the rosary to connect them.[8] Denis Keane went to the Spa RIC barracks, from where he phoned Ballymullen barracks, via the GPO in Edward Street, Tralee. Meanwhile the Free State force was rapidly advancing towards Spa, suffering their first fatality, Pte Patrick Quinn, at Kilfenora.[9] The republicans tried to implement a holding action at Sammy's Rock, a 100-foot crag near Spa, where a small, hastily assembled group of fifteen to twenty republicans offered resistance, resulting in the death of one Free State soldier, Pte Edward Byrne, and the loss of John O'Sullivan of Castlegregory on the republican side.

At this point both John Joe Sheehy and Mike McGlynn had arrived to assess the strength of the force they faced. The republicans decided that the best they could do in the face of the advancing Free State troops, was to hold off the advance long enough to enable them to burn and destroy Ballymullen barracks to deny the government army use of the principal military base in Kerry. However, even here the fates were against them. No sooner had they set fire to one of the blocks than it became apparent that some of their own men who had come off guard duty were still sleeping within and frantic measures had to be taken to rescue them.

By 1.30 p.m. the main Free State column under O'Daly had reached the Rock Street–Pembroke Street junction in Tralee, where the republicans had closed the level-crossing gates, using them as a roadblock to delay their advance. Initially the republicans wounded some of the government troops and seized some of their rifles, but a swift detour by the Free Staters along the railway track quickly negated the effectiveness of this roadblock. Armed with a Lewis machine-gun, Michael Fitzgerald and Johnny O'Connor had taken up a firing position on the roof of Shamrock Mills and sprayed the advancing column with gunfire, wounding several soldiers. Army Medical Service stretcher-bearers, wearing large Red Cross armbands, attempting to tend to these wounded men, also came under fire. Without any concern for his own safety, O'Daly grabbed a large Red Cross flag and began waving it vigorously in the vain hope it would bring a cessation in the machine-gun fire. In the end orders were given to storm the Mills, which were successfully executed, but O'Connor and Fitzgerald had already escaped. The Rock Street encounter, which claimed the lives of six Dublin Guards and one medical orderly, would prove to be the largest single death toll the Free State army would suffer during the entire conflict in Kerry.

At Corporal Niall Harrington's suggestion, the remaining troops moved along Nelson Street, passing by Latchford's Mills, which luckily for the Free State had not been garrisoned in the manner John Joe Sheehy had suggested. Had it been, the resulting casualty levels to the government troops, from a combination of Lewis machine-gun, grenade and sniper fire, might well have been dozens (killed and wounded) given the evidence of their Rock Street experience.

In the late afternoon the vanguard of the Free State force approached Moyderwell barracks, where they chose to use rifle grenades to force the garrison to evacuate their positions. This left the road open to their final objective, Ballymullen barracks.

The 7 August edition of *Republican Bulletin* in the *Cork Examiner* went into overdrive when describing what happened next. It extolled the heroic efforts of a single republican armoured car as it gallantly offered resistance to two Free State armoured cars at Moyderwell Cross in an attempt to prevent them advancing on Ballymullen barracks. The report was pure fiction. It read more like an account of an American Civil War battle between 'Ironclads' (battleships) in the opening stages of that war than any actual confrontation in suburban Tralee during August 1922. The press release was equally wide of the mark in its report of the level of casualties inflicted on the government force by the republicans: 31 dead and over 100 wounded.[10] The *Army Bulletin* (an official source of information subject to time delays and military censorship) report on the Tralee operations, quoted in *The Irish Times* two days later, noted that 'seventy five-Irregulars – thirty a certainty – were killed during the capture of the town, while eleven National troops were killed and fourteen wounded in the same action'.[11] Tralee republicans who later read this version of events were bemused by the alleged death toll, which elicited the remark, 'there weren't seventy-five live republicans in Tralee that August, never mind seventy-five dead ones'.[12] Niall Harrington estimated that at most twenty to thirty national troops were wounded capturing Tralee, a figure that corresponds to Paddy Cahill's field report to Kerry No. 1 Brigade on the republican side.

While the fire the republicans had lit at Ballymullen had done some damage to the officer's mess, the most impressive building in the barracks, most of the other facilities were left unscathed and were quickly utilised by incoming troops. From a practical point of view the army set up over a dozen smaller posts in and around Tralee: at the Jeffers Institute, Day Place; at the corner of the Mall/Nelson Street; the Post Office, Edward Street; several locations on both Rock and Pembroke Street; and at Ballyard and Boherbee. All these positions ensured that they had effective 'on the ground' control over most of Tralee's urban area, as well as Ballymullen barracks, within days of the Fenit landings.

THE LANDING AT TARBERT

At 3 a.m. on Thursday 3 August, the *Corona* and three smaller boats left Kilrush, County Clare, bound for the coastal village of Tarbert. On board were 240 men drawn from the 1st Western

Division under the command of Colonel Michael Hogan.[13] The 1st Western Division evolved from the East Clare Brigade of the IRA following its reorganisation in the summer of 1921, and was ultimately under the command of Michael Brennan, a twenty-five-year-old from Meelick on the Clare–Limerick border. The bulk of the force was from Clare, but it also contained a sizeable contingent from south Galway. During the stand-off with Ernie O'Malley in Limerick in March 1922, the unit incorporated Limerick pro-Treaty troops into its ranks. The 1st Westerns were regarded, along with the Dublin Guards, as one of the most militarily effective and politically reliable units in the government's army, and the dispatch of both these units to Kerry is a clear indication of the importance Collins placed on bringing hostilities to a swift conclusion in the county.

Michael Hogan, aged twenty-two, a native of Kilfrikle, Loughrea, County Galway, was the son of a civil servant with the Land Commission, who farmed 270 acres in east Galway. He was from an academically gifted family and his eldest brother, Patrick Hogan (a solicitor by training), was appointed Minister for Agriculture in January 1922, a portfolio he retained until the Cumann na nGaedheal government left office in 1932. Another of Hogan's brothers, James, had served as intelligence officer of the East Clare Brigade during the War of Independence, a role he would go on to hold for the National Army for the duration of the Civil War, before taking up an appointment as professor of history at UCC at the end of hostilities.

Arriving in Tarbert, Colonel Hogan found that the anti-Treaty garrison had left town, leaving the charred ruins of the coastguard station in their wake to deprive the incoming force of accommodation and a headquarters. Leaving twenty-five troops under the command of Captain Brian O'Grady and Lieutenant Egan billeted in the RIC barracks, the unit moved on to Ballylongford, where they took six republican prisoners and captured their arms and ammunition.

The main force entered Listowel at 5.30 p.m. without meeting any resistance and took some additional prisoners, bringing their total tally (including those arrested in Ballylongford) to twenty-three.[14] The republicans had abandoned the town, leaving the workhouse, the courthouse and the RIC barracks as burnt-out shells. An additional fifty troops, under the command of Captain Matthew McGrath (aged twenty-one) from Feakle, east Clare, were billeted in the town. Combined with the earlier deployment in Tarbert, these troops represented more than a quarter of the original force, and meant that a large proportion of Hogan's troops were now restricted to static positions. The civilian population of Listowel were glad to see the troops enter their town, as their arrival brought to an end months of virtual isolation, which had seriously reduced the levels of trade and commerce between the town and its rural hinterland.

By nightfall the remainder of Hogan's column had arrived in Ballymullen barracks, linking up with O'Daly's forces. At the end of day two of the landings almost 700 government troops were in situ in north Kerry and Tralee in what might be described as a political and military vacuum, and with very little local knowledge.

The *Lady Wicklow* left Fenit on 4 August bound for Dublin, carrying the bodies of the troops who had been killed capturing the town. Michael Collins was among the attendees at their state funeral on 8 August. In a short letter to his fiancée, Kitty Kiernan, he wrote: 'The scenes at mass were really heartbreaking. The poor women weeping and almost shrieking (some of them) for their dead sons. Sisters, and one wife were there too, and a few small children. It makes one feel I tell you.'[15]

By this time the *Lady Wicklow*, with another boat called the *Avaronia*, were on their way to Cork, where they would land troops at Union Hall (180), Youghal (200) and Passage West (800) as part of a highly successful series of coastal incursions on the 'rebel county' from 8–9 August. The only concerted republican resistance occurred at Rochestown (leaving nine Free State soldiers and seven republicans dead), which simply postponed the capture of the southern capital by one day, leaving it in government hands by 11 August 1922.

CONSOLIDATING THE LANDINGS

Also on 4 August, Eamon Horan, the only senior IRA figure from Tralee to take a pro-Treaty stance, began a recruitment campaign to enlist a 'Kerry Brigade' to serve and broaden the government's military presence in the county. The majority of the recruits, whose principal military asset at this point was their knowledge of Tralee and its hinterland, under Horan's direction assisted the Dublin Guards in searching for and rounding up known republicans. This brought the number of detainees in government hands to around 100, including the forty or so captured on the first day of fighting. Among the prisoners was twenty-five-year-old Billy Mullins, brigade quartermaster, Kerry

No. 1 Brigade. Describing the conditions during an earlier stay in Tralee Gaol, he noted:

> Tralee Gaol had a dank, musty odour from the moment one entered it. It was most noticeable from the cells and bedding, blankets etc. I heard many hard remarks on its condition by my fellow prisoners. It did not seem so bad to me as I knew the inside of the place since I had often served mass there when I was an altar boy at St John's Parish Church.[16]

These remarks relate to Mullins' incarceration in the jail in the wake of the 1916 Rising, but conditions would not have changed much between 1916 and 1922.

Early on Saturday morning, 5 August, a combined force of the Dublin Guards and the 1st Westerns commanded by James Dempsey and James McGuinness, left Tralee for Farranfore. Taking advantage of the arrival of Hogan's men from Listowel, Paddy O'Daly had decided to extend the area under the government's control. In this regard he was following the strategy that Collins and Mulcahy had outlined for undermining the Munster Republic. Collins realised that an immediate overwhelming defeat of the republicans was unlikely, so a practical strategy would be to establish a military presence in the principal towns in the area. As the army presence expanded and daily life in the area returned to normal as a consequence, local people would see the government as a positive force in their lives. Gradually the republican heartland would shrink, and the pro-government enclave would expand from the inside out.

Unsure of what levels of resistance they would encounter,

the force included their 18-pounder field gun in their arsenal. The soldiers' arrival took the local garrison at Farranfore totally by surprise. The Free State troops would later recall jokingly that the republican garrison not only abandoned their arms and ammunition in their haste to avoid capture, but also left their half-eaten dinners on the table. Unable to find any 'Irregulars' (as the government and the press increasingly dubbed them) in the follow-up search, the Free State troops returned to the deserted headquarters and duly ate the abandoned dinners.[17]

The republican outpost on the approaches to Castleisland, the Free State troops' next target, offered more stubborn resistance, but the discharge of a number of shells from the 18-pounder proved the decisive factor, forcing the defenders to abandon the outpost. The use of artillery was as much a psychological weapon (and a warning salvo to future enemy encounters) as a military necessity. In Castleisland itself some of the republican garrison were trapped by the shelling and government troops claimed to have taken thirty republicans prisoner.[18] Both Farranfore and Castleisland were in government hands by 12.30 p.m. From a republican perspective, the local garrisons were too small and had insufficient quantities of ammunition to offer a credible resistance that would inflict serious casualties on the attacking troops. In the face of this much stronger force, to stand and fight would ultimately involve being surrounded, captured and removed from the equation for the remainder of the conflict.

Though much smaller in terms of population than Castle-island, Farranfore represented a key strategic asset due to its pivotal position in the county's rail and road network. Lying midway between Tralee and Killarney, and with 'spur' lines to

Castleisland and Valentia it provided the promise of swift lines of communication into central Kerry and the mountain vastness of the Iveragh peninsula. In early twentieth-century Ireland the rail network was vastly superior both in terms of standards of construction and speed of service than any comparable communications by road. Indeed for the duration of the conflict the GS&WR and, to a lesser extent, the Tralee and Dingle Railway Company, would see their rail tracks, bridges, signalling equipment, rolling stock, locomotives and stations repeatedly sabotaged and destroyed by republicans to deprive the National Army of a transport network that reached virtually every important population centre in Kerry. In the process the civilian population of the county was deprived of a cheap, speedy and efficient means of public transport with all the repercussions that its absence implied in the commercial, economic and social life of the community. It became more difficult to bring agricultural produce to the weekly market; basic foodstuffs, such as tea, sugar and salt, were not delivered to local shops; and postal deliveries were suspended. All of this combined to increase people's sense of isolation and make their daily lives a misery.

Of course the republicans did not consider the discomfort their campaign caused to members of the wider community, as they were by and large contemptuous of them – they felt themselves to be immune from public opinion or criticism. On 10 August, in spite of a well-organised protest campaign by commercial and municipal leaders on the impact its destruction would have on the local economy, republicans blew up a section of the Blackwater viaduct at Mallow, thereby severing rail contact between Cork city and the south-west and the rest of the country. It should be noted, however, the actual conflict rarely impacted on the ordinary person's sense of personal safety. Unlike other civil conflicts such as the Mexican Revolution or the Spanish Civil War, where popular support for both protagonists was extremely widespread and ran very deep, most of the civilian population were largely indifferent to the ideological fault lines of Free State versus Republic.

The positive side of this non-alignment was an almost total absence of any attacks or atrocities perpetrated against civilians by either side in Kerry. On the rare occasions where innocent bystanders were either killed or wounded, it was usually the result of coming under crossfire, or being caught up in an ambush or firefight between the two belligerents. Generally speaking, republican attacks were episodic and opportunistic, with government troop movements being under constant – but covert – surveillance by IRA scouts in rural areas; in towns, the younger Fianna Éireann or Cumann na mBan members passed on information which could result in a sniper, or one or two men with revolvers and/or hand grenades (popularly known as Mills bombs), opening fire on a foot patrol or an army vehicle on its return journey when they would know its route. Individual sentries and soldiers entering and leaving the relative safety of buildings also had to be wary of snipers. For district army patrols, a felled tree on the road could be a prelude to an ambush, or be booby-trapped to kill or maim any soldier who tried to remove the obstacle. As most of the government troops in Kerry were either serving in Dublin or Clare units, they had none of the local knowledge that their republican opponents had of the terrain and the locations the local IRA had used to their advantage in the war against the British little more than a year earlier.

It has often been stated that neighbour was reluctant to shoot neighbour, and this probably caused many ambushes to be aborted, resulting in low casualty levels in the Civil War. Indeed, some authorities state the 'outside' factor in Kerry – the fact that the bulk of the national troops, the Dublin Guards in particular, came from outside the county – was one of the chief reasons the conflict was so bitter there.[19] This is certainly a valid point, but the Civil War, both in Kerry and elsewhere in the country, was a conflict that bred maverick actions driven by the intensity of a vendetta. On 5–6 August three individual Kerrymen would lose their lives in incidents that were in many ways typical of the conflict in the county.

The actual details surrounding the death of Private Michael Purcell of No. 2, Lower Abbey Street, Tralee, are scant. It is known that he enlisted in the Kerry Brigade on 4 August as part of Eamon Horan's recruitment drive. In a staunchly republican town like Tralee the fact that he joined the hated Free State army was enough in someone's eyes to justify his death, which probably came from a sniper's bullet.

Michael Reidy, a seventeen-year-old Fianna member from Ballymacelligott, was observing an army patrol somewhere in the vicinity of the Earl of Desmond Hotel in Ballyseedy on Saturday 5 August, when unbeknownst to him he was spotted by one of the soldiers and summarily shot dead.[20] Most probably Michael Reidy was unarmed at the time he was killed.

The development of scattered outposts necessitated a supply network to deliver food and ammunition to the garrison, as well as facilitating the changing of the guard on a regular basis. The IRA had set up a surveillance network after losing Farranfore and Castleisland and was aware of this supply network. A supply lorry was ambushed at Knockeen Cross, on the way to Castleisland, resulting in the death of Captain Brian Houlihan of the Dublin Guards and the wounding of three others, two of whom would subsequently die of wounds inflicted by 'dum-dum' Mauser bullets, which fragmented on hitting bone, creating hideous shrapnel-type internal injuries. A native of Kenmare and a veteran of the 1916 Rising and the War of Independence, Houlihan, who had travelled to Kerry on board the *Lady Wicklow*, was the first of seventeen troops who would die in Kerry while engaged in convoy protection duties, either delivering supplies to isolated army posts or escorting humanitarian deliveries of basic foodstuffs to aid the hard-pressed civilian population in Tralee and Killarney.[21]

THE LANDING AT KENMARE

On 7 August 1922, the *Cork Examiner* carried a report from the *New York Times* of an explosion damaging the transatlantic cable link at the Waterville station owned by the Commercial Cable Company. No details are given as to when the bombing occurred, but given the time lag between Europe and America in the 1920s the incident probably occurred in late July. The 1 August edition included an account of an incident that may have been connected to the Waterville explosion:

On Saturday a party attempted a landing from a British war sloop on the Kenmare river. Republican forces opened fire on them forcing them to withdraw and return to their ship. Later seven shells were fired at Lickeen coastguard station. Two hit the building. Republicans returned rifle fire for 400 yards.

On 10 August General Dermot McManus arranged to have two vessels, the *Mermaid* and the *Margaret*, at the dockside in Limerick city to transport Brigadier Tom O'Connor Scarteen and the 250 men under his command to Kenmare. John Linge, writing in 'The British navy and the Irish Civil War', takes the view that the Kenmare landing was influenced in part by Collins' wish to mollify Churchill's concern that the Valentia cable station (a vital British national interest for both commercial and military traffic, in Churchill's opinion) be protected from republican sabotage.[22] Of course Collins may not have told Brigadier Tom O'Connor, the task force leader, of Churchill's personal concern in the mission.

The majority of the men in O'Connor's force were new recruits, the bulk of them from Cork (Cobh and Youghal) and Kerry (east Kerry No. 2 area), who had recently seen action in east Limerick in the Bruff, Bruree and Kilmallock salient.[23] There was also a sprinkling of men from the more experienced Northern Division, as well as a younger brother of Kevin O'Higgins, the Provisional Government's Justice Minister. Brigadier O'Connor (aged twenty-four) was the only commander of any significance in Kerry from the War of Independence days to adopt a pro-Treaty position. Bertie Scully of Rossbeigh suggested that O'Connor took this stance because of the fact that he had been passed over as brigade engineer when the IRA was reorganised over the summer of 1921.[24] Whether this was the case or not, O'Connor was a formidable addition to the government's military force, given both his knowledge of his adversaries (former comrades) in the Kerry No. 2 and No. 3 Brigades, and his familiarity with the topography of south Kerry, which was ideal ambush country with its wild coastal and mountain terrain.

During the voyage down from Limerick, McManus, a Mayo man and a graduate of Sandhurst Military Academy, who served with the Royal Enniskillen Fusiliers at Gallipoli, was not impressed by either the calibre or the discipline of the men on board, recalling, 'even on the ship I had a good deal of friction with those young fellows'.[25]

Uncertain of the scale of the republican force occupying Kenmare, O'Connor put ashore in a rowing boat at Conngar harbour, and headed towards the coastguard station at Lickeen, about three miles away, which was garrisoned by a force of about thirty men. Returning to the *Margaret*, O'Connor was preparing to bring a landing party ashore when her sister ship, the *Mermaid*, saw smoke billowing further up the Kenmare river. Sailing in the direction of the smoke they reported that the republicans had abandoned the post and set it on fire.

Brigadier O'Connor's flotilla approached the entrance to the Kenmare river at about 5.30 p.m. on Friday 11 August 1922. There were still republicans on the pier where the stone parapet offered good cover, and had the defending garrison chosen to, they could have inflicted substantial casualties on the incoming force with little cost to themselves.[26] Instead they abandoned the town, allowing O'Connor's force to occupy Kenmare without opposition.

McManus had advised the men that after landing they should take up defensive positions around the perimeter of the town, garrison the barracks properly and carry out regular patrols of the town. However, no sooner had they arrived in Kenmare than they went visiting and drinking with their friends, seeing themselves as returning 'home' with all the negative connotations that had for their efficiency as an occupying force. They were after all still in territory occupied by a hostile force. Tom O'Connor returned to his uncle's family home over the bakery at No. 5 Main Street without posting a sentry to guard what was in effect the Command HQ, while the remaining troops billeted themselves at the workhouse, the Carnegie Library and the National Bank.

According to the *Cork Examiner*, the troops were given an enthusiastic welcome by the townspeople of Kenmare, and the Church parade on Sunday 13 August, where the troops marched in uniform but unarmed to mass, was a spectacular scene never before seen in Kenmare. The splendid military bearing of the troops was a cause of great celebration and excitement. Archdeacon Patrick Marshall, parish priest of Kenmare, welcomed the troops to the town and used the occasion to condemn the republicans for the destruction of the coastguard station at Lickeen, as well as the RIC barracks and the fever hospital in Kenmare. The burning of the latter drew particular criticism, as Marshall pointed out that while the building was not now in use, it might be needed in the future in the event of outbreaks of serious illnesses or diseases that might require isolation to contain their infection from the wider community.[27]

Within a few days of arriving in Tralee, Colonel David Neligan, Collins' director of intelligence in Kerry, had made contact through an intermediary with Paddy Cahill, with the intention of entering into discussions to bring about an end to hostilities in Kerry.

Cahill said that unless Billy Mullins and Paddy Paul Fitzgerald, Tralee republicans captured on 2 August who were confidants of Cahill, were part of the negotiating team, no discussions were possible. Fitzgerald and Mullins were still incarcerated in Tralee.[28] On Saturday 12 August, Michael Collins visited Tralee as part of a wider tour of the south-west. Given the fall of Cork city, and the capture of Kenmare the previous day, he must have been pleased how quickly Free State forces had ruptured the hull of the Munster Republic. With landings at Tarbert on the Shannon at one end and Youghal on the Cork–Waterford border at the other, as well as several intermediate points in between over the course of ten days, the idea of a republican heartland in the south now seemed delusional to all but the most militaristic and doctrinaire republicans. Collins had prepared the ground for discussions on peace via Neligan's preliminary overtures.

While in Tralee, Collins received news of the death of Arthur Griffith in Dublin and cut short his plans for discussions, returning to the capital. The rapid capture of several key towns in Kerry within a few days of Collins' visit suggests that the instructions he left were pretty specific: continue to expand the area in Kerry under the government's control. Even had talks taken place it is highly improbable that the war in Kerry would have come to an end at this point. The republicans would have viewed Collins' sea operations as a clever – if underhand – way of gaining an advantage while they were unable to defend themselves. As far as they were concerned their campaign was only beginning.

It would be extremely premature to dismiss republican resistance in Kerry as a spent force at this point. At 4 p.m. on 12 August a twenty-five-man patrol of 1st Westerns returning from transporting prisoners to Tarbert for transfer by boat to Limerick, reached a particularly exposed stretch of road at Bedford, on the approach to Listowel, when they came under Thompson submachine-gun fire from republicans. John Quayne, from Meelick, County Clare, was killed and two others were wounded, before the sound of gunfire drew the 'Ex Mutineer' armoured car to the scene, where it focused concentrated machine-gun fire on the republicans. Its arrival gave the Free State troops (whose ammunition stocks, with the exception of Captain McGrath's rifle, were virtually depleted) the opportunity to take cover and in the process seriously reduced the casualty levels that would have otherwise occurred.[29] The 'Ex Mutineer's' gunner afterwards claimed to have wounded seven republicans.[30]

CHAPTER 3

GAINING GROUND, HOLDING GROUND

Free State troops, predominantly Dublin Guards, commanded by James Dempsey and James McGuinness, must have felt a degree of trepidation on Sunday 13 August, as they approached Killarney. If they were to believe their own propaganda, as reported in *The Irish Times*, the town was occupied by a force of over 500 'Irregulars' commanded by Erskine Childers.[1] On the face of it, the idea that such a large concentration of republicans – virtually half of all the IRA active in Kerry – would risk being surrounded and captured en masse while defending Killarney is absurd, and it goes against the grain of all the previous tactics adopted by the IRA both in Kerry and elsewhere. Republican strongholds such as Limerick and Cork, cities far more strategically valuable than Killarney, had been abandoned without any serious attempts being made to implement a coherent evacuation of these urban centres as a way of inflicting maximum casualties on the National Army.

On the other hand, as Killarney was the headquarters of Kerry No. 2 Brigade, the republicans in the town might be expected to defend their town more robustly than Kerry No. 1 Brigade had done at Tralee ten days earlier. On that occasion national troops had the advantage of a surprise attack, but nevertheless a single Lewis gun had inflicted relatively high casualties on the Dublin Guards in the Pembroke–Rock Street area of the town. In the interim, towns like Listowel and Castleisland had been taken without any serious fighting; but the Kerry republicans in Killarney had time to prepare the town's defences and absorb the Kerry contingents that were returning from the Limerick front to rejoin their local units. Finally, the presence of Erskine Childers as commander would help galvanise the defending garrison.

Childers, in many ways a *bête noir* of the Free State army, was portrayed as a military genius. He had served in the Boer War and had written a highly acclaimed text book on guerrilla warfare based on those experiences. He had also written the prophetic novel, *Riddle of the Sands*, a 'Boys Own'-type adventure warning of the dangers to Britain of the German naval build-up in the North Sea. He had then turned full circle and used his yacht, the *Asgard*, to smuggle German rifles into Howth in 1914 to arm the Irish Volunteers. And yet, Childers' reputation as military leader was based as much on his ability to hold a pen as it was to shoulder a rifle; indeed his principal role during the Civil War was to return good copy as a propagandist in the pro-republican *War News*.

In war, as in all other areas of human activity, what people believe to be true is as important as the actual truth in determining their actions. And so, the final advance on Killarney took place under the cover of darkness to minimise the number of potential casualties the National Army might incur in capturing the town. In the event government troops occupied Killarney at 11 p.m. on

Sunday night, to discover that only about sixty of the 'original' force (estimated between 400 and 700) remained in the town. This figure was probably close to the real strength of the garrison actually based in Killarney. As they abandoned the town the republicans burned down the RIC barracks and the 'new' Great Southern Hotel (built in 1907, to cater for those who could not afford the more luxurious older establishment), so as to deprive the incoming troops of accommodation. The older part of the hotel, opened in 1854 and consisting of over 100 bedrooms, was spared destruction thanks to the intervention of Séan Moylan, the republican 'director of operations'.[2] The Great Southern was the lynchpin of Killarney's tourist industry, and the destruction of a facility that was the jewel in the crown of Kerry tourism would take the town years, if not decades, to recover from an action which would have resulted in the loss of a quarter of the town's most deluxe accommodation.

According to a report in the *Kerry People*, the townspeople of Killarney declared Monday 14 August a bank holiday to mark their 'liberation'. Interestingly, neither the local press, nor any of the national dailies had any reports of casualties on anything like the scale that both sides had issued on the numbers of killed and wounded they inflicted on the enemy during the capture of Tralee. The *Kerry People* was the only newspaper still in operation in the county at the start of the Civil War. An eight-page weekly newspaper owned and edited by Maurice Ryle, it gave balanced and accurate coverage of the conflict, but its independent editorial line would not have endeared it to republicans. National newspapers such as the *Freeman's Journal*, *The Irish Times* and the *Irish Independent* (which were read by few people in Kerry at the best of times), as well as the *Cork Examiner*, would have become unavailable from mid August onwards once the conflict cut off rail and other means of communications between Kerry and the rest of the country. The *Kerry People*'s last edition rolled off the press on Saturday 26 August 1922 – a day or two later republicans visited the *Kerry People* print works and removed the main printing press, causing the newspaper to cease publication.[3] Maurice Ryle would later submit a compensation claim of £1,050 for the loss of the equipment. It would probably be more difficult to put a price on the loss of press freedom.

On Wednesday 16 August, a detachment of Dublin Guards left Killarney bound for Rathmore. There they found the republicans had abandoned the town leaving their customary 'burnt offering' – the charred remains of the RIC barracks – for the incoming troops. The local courthouse was used as temporary accommodation and troops were also billeted in a number of private houses. The next day, Thursday 17 August, about 100 men from the 1st Westerns left Tralee. En route to Killorglin they set up an outpost at Castlemaine, before moving on to Milltown. The column encountered some resistance near Kilderry, between Milltown and Killorglin, but it was half-hearted, and the government force took six republicans prisoner, capturing their arms and ammunition. Arriving in Killorglin, the Free State troops were cordially received and cheered by townspeople. A sixty-man force commanded by Captain Donal Lehane (aged twenty-four), a veteran of the War of Independence from Lahinch, County Clare, was divided in three.[4] Lehane selected Morris's Hotel as his command headquarters, primarily because of its proximity to Saint James' church, whose square tower (accessible independently of the church building) provided an ideal observation point/machine-gun post with its commanding views of the town and the rail and road approaches from Tralee and Killarney. The remaining troops, commanded by Lieutenant O'Callaghan from Kilfenora, County Clare, took over Killorglin RIC barracks, which had been partially damaged by a landmine detonated by the evacuating garrison. The Carnegie Library, which also served as the town's secondary school, was placed under the command of Lieutenant Corry.

At this point, the Dublin Guards had assumed responsibility for the Kerry No. 2 Brigade area in the eastern part of the county, while the 1st Westerns presided over north Kerry and the rural areas of the Kerry No. 1 Brigade. Both units had a presence in Ballymullen barracks and patrolled both the Tralee urban area and its hinterland. By mid August the Free State army did not yet have any foothold on the Dingle peninsula; but anticipating Dingle would be next on their list, the local republican garrison burned down both the town's RIC barracks and its coastguard station.

From his base in Kenmare, Tom O'Connor Scarteen and his second-in-command, Captain Dick O'Sullivan, commandeered a meal and flour boat (a 600-ton coaster from Limerick) and, with 100 men on board, sailed up the coast to Reenard Point. Michael Christopher (Dan) O'Shea provides an interesting account of the voyage and manoeuvres:

> The troopship reached Valentia Harbour before noon, Wednesday 23 and troops occupied the island with its transatlantic cable station. Then on to the mainland at Reenard Point, moving up Reenard road, leading up to Cahirciveen, about a mile to the

east. While the 'Scarteen' troops were regrouping for their thrust into Cahirciveen they came under rifle fire from the thirty or so anti-Treaty volunteers who evacuated the town at about 3 p.m. when they became aware of the landing. The fusillade was largely ineffective and the soldiers returned fire and eight riflemen, a Lewis gunner and a local guide went up to engage the withdrawing force on Knockeen road. It was now twilight and engagements were called off as dwelling houses were in the line of fire. Brigadier O'Connor occupied Cahirciveen via West End, New Street, in the early hours of 24 August and immediately set up posts and billets. Save for one motorcycle they had brought on the troopship the column had no motorised transport. O'Connor requisitioned five Model Ts in Cahirciveen, all of which had been dismantled by the withdrawing force. Fortunately for Scarteen, Bill Ower, a Scotsman and a mechanical genius, had the motors in running order by Friday afternoon, ready to embark on a thrust to take Waterville 10 miles away. With Scarteen driving the leading car, the five Model Ts set out for Waterville about 8 p.m. with his batman Sergeant Jack O'Donovan riding the motorcycle alongside. With four men to each car and two extra standing on the running boards, as well as half a dozen on push bikes, their armament, Lee Enfield rifles and a Lewis gun, one of three brought to Cahirciveen, Waterville was taken over without incident at 10 p.m. Many of the three dozen or so troops engaged in the Waterville advance were Cahirciveen volunteers who joined up when the town was taken.[5]

In Waterville troops were billeted at the Butler Arms Hotel. Even though O'Connor had recruited some additional troops and gained a motorised 'wing' during the Cahirciveen operations

– thereby increasing his force's mobility considerably – it was apparent to him that his force was far too small to be effective, especially as he was now providing garrisons on Valentia Island, Cahirciveen and Waterville as well as Kenmare, while at the same time trying to maintain a presence in Kerry No. 2 and Kerry No. 3 Brigade areas. The sense of geographic isolation and the lack of communication with other parts of Kerry command must have given troops stationed in south Kerry the feeling that they were part of a forgotten army.

While abandoning the main population centres to national troops, the republicans mounted a concerted campaign aimed at destroying rail communications in the county, so as to force all military traffic onto the roads and enable the anti-Treaty side to have much greater freedom in deciding ambush locations. In early August rails were taken up between Tralee and Farranfore and at several points on the thirty-nine-mile Farranfore–Valentia line, while bridges were blown up at Ballycarthy and Ballyseedy, and burned at Headford Junction and near Kenmare. A landmine detonated under a moving train derailed a locomotive and some carriages between Ballyhar and Farranfore. There were also more subtle ways of undermining the rail network. During the War of Independence many rail employees mounted a non co-operation campaign, refusing to handle any military traffic including both men and materials. This solidarity continued in Kerry, manifesting itself during the early stages of the Civil War in support of the republican cause. For example GS&WR employees dismantled fourteen railway engines in Tralee station. In reaction to this, eight rail workers were arrested by the army, who replaced the crucial parts of the locomotives that had been removed.[6]

As the campaign progressed republicans took a more aggressive approach. On Monday 14 August at 5 p.m. they ambushed a train at Curran's Bridge near Farranfore. A small landmine detonated on the line in front of the train brought it to a halt, whereupon rifle fire concentrated on the locomotive wounded both the driver, Denis O'Keeffe, and the guard, Daniel Linehan, as well as the soldier 'riding shotgun', twenty-year-old Joseph Berry of Clifton, County Galway. Among the passengers on the train were Paddy O'Daly and James McGuinness, the government's most senior military men in Kerry, and a couple of American journalists, for whom the encounter must have contained echoes of the 'Wild West'. The train's defences also included a machine-gun post, and once the gunner identified the source of the rifle fire, he concentrated his fire on that area, causing the ambush to be aborted. In the follow-up search, an Irregular named O'Connor was captured and 600 yards of cable, three landmines and three detonators were seized.[7]

The next day, Tuesday 15 August, republicans held up a break-down train returning from Killarney to Tralee. The team had repaired damaged track and the rail bridge at Killan, when they were fired upon by Irregulars and forced to destroy the repairs. On the return journey the train, a locomotive and two carriages, slowed down at Ballymacthomas, about five miles from Tralee, to allow a GS&WR employee to get off the train. As it did so, Mr Carroll, the Permanent Way Inspector, the driver and the fireman were taken at gunpoint and ordered to drive at full speed to Tralee. All three refused to carry out the republicans' command. As it turned out, one of the republicans – an ex-GS&WR employee – knew how to operate the locomotive and commandeered the train, proceeding towards Tralee at speeds of between fifty and sixty miles per hour. As it approached the station, disaster was averted thanks to the swift response of Johnny O'Connor, a GS&WR employee, who manually switched the tracks, thereby diverting the train from the main station. The train smashed into a buffer, crashed into three stationary goods wagons and ploughed through two solid masonry walls before plunging across the Listowel road where the boiler ruptured and reduced the two wagons to matchwood close to houses occupied by railway workers.[8] Fortunately there were no people either in the railway station or on the Listowel road when the locomotive exploded, which was initially assumed by those who heard it to be a bomb explosion.

Public opinion was appalled by the recklessness of the republican actions, while it prompted the GS&WR to suspend all rail services, effective from Friday 18 August. Two days later the company announced it would pay off its entire permanent staff (including clerical grades) effective from 22 August. This involved substantial job losses in Kerry as the GS&WR employed sixty-four staff in the Tralee district, nine in Killarney and thirty-eight in Cahirciveen.[9] For the Great Southern and Western Railway, a private company, it was a black week. The loss of the new Great Southern Hotel and the destruction of the locomotive cost the company £30,000 and £15,000 respectively.[10]

Viewed from a strictly military perspective the republican campaign on the Great Southern and Western front was a great success. Liam Lynch, Chief-of-Staff of the IRA and O/C 1st Southern Division, in a short memo to Ernie O'Malley, dated 18 August 1922, remarked: 'The situation in Kerry is everything that could be desired. Pressure is so great that the enemy were forced to evacuate Farranfore, an important junction, and return to their base in Tralee.'[11]

Due to the conflict, the only guests the company was now likely to have in the Great Southern Hotel, Killarney, were soldiers of the Free State army. For the Dublin Guards lucky enough to be billeted in the hotel, with its high Victorian décor echoing Georgian influences and its Corinthian-columned dining room, their immediate surroundings were a world away from most army accommodation and must have added a surreal quality to their experience of Killarney. For the hotel staff, there must have been a sense of *déjà vu*, as it was little more than six months since over 500 members of the British army's Royal Fusiliers Regiment had vacated the premises after a residency spanning two years. Many republicans claimed that although a green uniform had replaced a khaki one, it made little difference. They referred to the National Army as 'Green and Tans', a term of contempt. As they saw it the Provisional Government was only a puppet administration beholden to Lloyd George and its army a barely disguised repackaging of the recently disbanded 'Irish' regiments of the British army.[12]

On Thursday 17 August, two medical orderlies, Privates Cecil Fitzgerald and John O'Meara from Gort and Galway city respectively, had a day off from their duties in Killarney and decided to walk to Ross Castle. Aged sixteen and twenty respectively, and wearing their army uniforms with large Red Cross badges on their upper arms, they asked Robert Roberts, a local boatman, to ferry them out to Innisfallen Island from the castle grounds. As the two medics stepped onto the pier at Innisfallen, they were both shot dead by a sniper firing from the island. Fearing for his own life, Roberts dived for cover and then returned to the mainland, where he alerted the military authorities to what had happened. The army carried out a thorough search of Innisfallen, but those responsible for the double killing had long since left the island.[13]

People in Killarney were shocked by the deaths of the two soldiers, both because of the men's relative youth and the fact that they were unarmed and on a tourist trip at the time of their deaths. Father Jarlath, speaking at mass in the Franciscan Friary later that evening, was unequivocal in his condemnation of the republican attack. He described 'the brutality and callousness of a foul deed which is not justified in lawful warfare, and considering the Irish Bishops' pronouncement on armed resistance to the supreme authority of the will of the Irish people. The commission of such a crime would not be tolerated or carried out even by uncivilised tribes.' (The Bishops' pronouncement declared that the republicans had no moral right to challenge the Provisional Government's authority.) He finished his homily by telling the congregation that, at the request of the people of Killarney, 7 p.m. masses at the Franciscan Friary for the next two weeks would be offered for the repose of the souls of Fitzgerald and O'Meara.[14]

On Friday 18 August, a large motorised column left Killarney for Rathmore with the twin aims of consolidating the foothold they had established there a few days earlier and carrying out a wider reconnaissance of the east Kerry area. The importance of the patrol to the National Army was reflected by the fact that the convoy was commanded by both Brigadier Paddy O'Daly and Colonel James McGuinness, the two most senior officers in the Dublin Guards, and included an armoured car and an 18-pounder field gun in its arsenal as a contingency in the event of a major confrontation with the enemy. The republicans decided to ambush the convoy, seeing it as the thin edge of the wedge, and reckoning a strong assault would be the best way to deter further incursions into a salient that was for them a safe area. In fact, the sinewy roads that wound around the Clydagh valley and along the edges of the Derrynasaggart mountains were part of a republican enclave that stretched from east Kerry across the Cork border as far east as Ballyvourney and Macroom; it would remain a no-go area for the Free State army right up to the end of hostilities in May 1923.

We are fortunate to have a first-hand account of the ambush from both a republican perspective as well as the pro-government newspaper coverage provided by the army. Jeremiah Murphy, fighting on the republican side, noted the ambush party consisted of seventy riflemen.[15] As the total pool of active republicans in east Kerry at this time was about 100 men, an attack of this strength represented a no-holds-barred assault, with every available rifle being committed to the fray.

The convoy reached Barraduff about 3 p.m. and divided in two, with part of the column, which included marching troops, under O'Daly's command continuing on towards Rathmore, while a touring car with Red Cross markings (indicating that it was designated as an ambulance) followed by several lorries drove in the direction of Headford. Jeremiah Murphy observed that all the soldiers in the touring car carried rifles, an infringement on the vehicle's use as an ambulance.[16] According to terms of the Geneva Convention such vehicles were forbidden to transport either armed troops, weapons or ammunition. Anticipating that the convoy would cross Droum Bridge, the republicans hastily began work on a trench that would halt the column at a point that provided the best target for their riflemen positioned along the hillside at points between 200 and 600 yards above the road. Time constraints meant that two of the republicans, Jerry Kennedy and Tim Daly, were still putting the final touches to the trench when the touring car/ambulance (with Colonel James McGuinness among its passengers) stopped and troops got out and began filling in the trench.

At this point Kennedy and Daly (senior officers in the East Kerry IRA) inadvertently walked out in front of the troops filling in the trench, and were fired upon on the assumption they were leading an attack. The republicans returned fire and wounded four soldiers, including Colonel McGuinness, who was hit in the head and bled profusely.[17] He was pulled to safety by Lieutenant Reddy, who completed filling in the trench. Meanwhile, Daly and Kennedy, carrying the rifles they had captured from the wounded men, returned to their own lines, forcing their men to hold their fire at a point that was very opportune for the government troops.

Having heard the gunfire from the Rathmore road, O'Daly's troops soon arrived on the scene, and all hell broke loose as Kennedy and Daly were now out of the line of fire. Amid the din and confusion twenty-one-year-old Corporal Niall Harrington held his nerve and correctly identified the source of the gunfire. The armoured car's Vickers machine-gun concentrated its fire on the areas pinpointed by Harrington, while the 18-pounder discharged a few shells in the same direction. Harrington's action would see him promoted from Corporal to Second Lieutenant, one of a few occasions that a field promotion occurred in Kerry during the Civil War.[18]

According to Jeremiah Murphy the republicans suffered no casualties, but their attack was stopped in its tracks by 'superior numbers and armaments'. Murphy took a degree of satisfaction from the fact that the Droum ambush was the only occasion that a field gun was used in his locality, in itself a compliment of sorts to the seventy riflemen. As they left the scene the Free State column abandoned two lorries, which the republicans duly burned. This seems a very short-sighted response, as retaining the lorries for their own use would have given the republicans much needed mobility in their campaign at a time when motorised transport was both a scarce and valuable commodity. Niall Harrington recalled that the Droum ambush, and the earlier shelling of Castleisland on 5 August, were the only occasions artillery was used during the Kerry campaign.[19]

The element of surprise – central to the success of the action – was gone, as the republicans understandably held their fire to allow two of their senior commanders to return to their own lines. The capture of arms and ammunition from wounded soldiers was such an integral part of republican ambush strategy that it was second nature not to miss an opportunity to augment their arsenal. Had Kennedy and Daly left immediately and not collected the rifles, the Droum ambush might have been more successful from the republicans' perspective.

At 8 p.m. on the same evening as the Droum ambush, four soldiers escorting a prisoner between Fenit and Tralee were challenged by republicans near Dan Lyons' pub in Spa, which was used as an outpost by the National Army. Sergeant Jack Lydon of James Street, Tralee, challenged the republicans on his own, allowing the three other men in the patrol to escape, but he was hit in the head and died on the spot. He was twenty-eight years old and had arrived in Tralee with the Dublin Guards on 2 August. According to Niall Harrington, four republicans took part in the attack, including Jim Walsh of Churchill and George Nagle of Castlemaine.[20]

Also on Friday 18 August, the same day as the Droum ambush and Spa attack, a number of cars laden with flour, bacon, sugar and other foodstuffs were stopped at Dromduhig about three miles from Killarney and held up by Irregulars, who took them away.[21] This was the first report of a republican hold-up of a food convoy. These hold-ups were used to provide food for IRA columns, who also used the seizures to supply foodstuffs to 'safe houses' giving shelter and assistance to republicans. However, their actions deprived the civilian population of Killarney of essential supplies. By early September the practice had become so widespread that public opinion demanded a solution. Consequently the military felt compelled to provide an armed escort to protect the convoys. During the course of the war a quarter of all Free State army deaths in Kerry would take place while on convoy escorts.

Against this wider backdrop of political violence, ordinary crime received scant media coverage and little attention from the civil authorities. In the vacuum provided by the absence of law and order, Tralee in particular experienced a spate of burglaries and armed robberies. A delegation of Tralee businessmen sought help from the municipal authority to set up a police force, possibly carrying out joint patrols with the military. Mr T. Huggard, the municipal solicitor, met the delegation and cautioned against joint civilian/military patrols, lest an attack on 'police' might lead to compensation claims against the local authority, who would presumably administer the *ad hoc* force until a more stable political environment would allow the deployment of a regular police force. If the patrols operated in tandem with the military (who would be armed) in the volatile political environment, the risk to the civilian members would be very high. Even if the patrols were exclusively civilian in composition, wearing a uniform, especially when on night patrol, would place them at risk of being taken for government troops by republicans. Tralee town and its surroundings was, in August 1922 and for several months afterwards, one of the most dangerous military postings in Kerry. Surprisingly no one in a decision-making position in military circles in Tralee considered introducing a curfew at this point – if only as away of protecting civilians. The measure was finally introduced in late October.

There were over a dozen outposts in and around Tralee, and with prisoner escorts, guard changing and the duty (often tedious) of manning static lookout points, there were plentiful targets for republicans, either for a lone sniper or two or three men with revolvers and hand grenades. Government troops increasingly used darkness for camouflage, to avoid giving their republican adversaries a clear target. The republicans adapted their tactics accordingly, with a degree of recklessness and often with consequences they hadn't intended.

At midnight on 21 August, two soldiers escorting a prisoner between Ballymullen barracks and the county jail at Moyderwell, were stalked by republicans. When the republicans threw their grenades they wounded two civilians, John George Foley and Thomas Horan, a cattle dealer from Ballymullen, mistaking them for the military patrol.[22]

Later that morning, about 4 a.m. on Tuesday 22 August, presumably the same unit that carried out the midnight attack, hearing a lot of talking and the sounds of revving engines at the 'Green', near one of the gates at Ballymullen barracks, assumed a large convoy was about to leave the barracks. In conditions of total darkness they lobbed five hand grenades over the wall to initiate the assault, following up the explosions with concentrated rifle and revolver fire. The number of casualties ensuing from the rifle fire was reduced as a consequence of Captain James Burke and Lieutenant Timothy McMahon's shouts to soldiers and prisoners alike to dive to the ground. The bulk of the men (105) in the convoy were republican prisoners, who were being escorted by a relatively small army patrol to the canal basin, from where they were to be transported by boat to Limerick. Fortunately for all concerned, two of the five grenades failed to explode, but those that did wounded five prisoners and three soldiers. One of the soldiers, Private John Galworthy of Inisboffin, County Galway, and a prisoner, Thomas Drummond (25), a married man with four children, living at 32 Rea Street, Tralee, and a labourer at O'Donovan's Mills, were seriously injured, suffering multiple shrapnel wounds. Galworthy died at the County Infirmary on Thursday 24 August, while Drummond lost his fight for life at the Bon Secours hospital later that same day.[23]

While the margin for error in republican attacks was much greater in the Tralee urban area after dark than elsewhere in Kerry, it could not be said with any degree of certainty that it was safe to drive the roads of Kerry even in broad daylight. In mid August, Edmund Burke, an Irish-American who lived in New York, but originally came from Miltown Malbay in County Clare, returned to Ireland for the first time in thirty-two years. As he drove over Headley's Bridge he was fired upon by republicans who assumed his Ford was the advance scout car that travelled ahead of a motorised column. Privately owned motor cars were extremely rare in Kerry at this time, and as army officers often used their own vehicles, in nine cases out of ten the assumption that the car was the advance vehicle would be an accurate one. Unfortunately for Edmund Burke he was the exception that proved the rule, and his wounds were serious enough to necessitate amputating his arm. A bystander who stood watching as the car drove by was also slightly wounded in the attack.[24] Commenting on the incident, Colonel Michael Hogan noted he had been fired upon at the same spot a few days earlier and that the shots were usually used as a signal to the rest of the ambush party to ready themselves for action.

Notwithstanding their setback the previous Friday afternoon at Droum Bridge, the Free State authorities appear to have acquired accurate intelligence on the republican command structure in east Kerry. Acting on this information, on Tuesday 22 August a small patrol commanded by Paddy O'Daly surrounded Michael Fleming's house in Kilcummin, believing it to be the republicans' east Kerry headquarters. O'Daly's challenge to the occupants to surrender elicited a hand grenade by way of a reply, which wounded a soldier named Grimes; O'Daly himself suffered a minor shrapnel wound in the thigh. Troops opened fire on the upper floor of the house, wounding a girl who had no political involvement. This persuaded the occupants to call 'cease fire', and six troops under Captain Conroy stormed the house, taking William Fleming, Con O'Leary, Daniel Mulvihill and Thomas

Daly (a first cousin of Dr Charles O'Sullivan, Bishop of Kerry) prisoner, as well as a number of other occupants of the house.[25]

During the follow-up search, troops confiscated six revolvers with 300 rounds of ammunition, three rifles with 100 rounds, a dozen hand grenades, a Ford car and several documents. As they made their way back to the road, the party came under fire from the very scouts that should have prevented them surrounding the house in the first place. Private Thomas Kavanagh of North Circular Road, Dublin, was shot dead and a prisoner named O'Brien was wounded. Later that same evening Captain Peadar O'Brien captured Patrick Allman near Farranfore in a shoot-out where it was claimed two republicans were killed.[26] Overall, it was a good day for Kerry command.

The Provisional Government lost its most important political and military leader, Michael Collins, as darkness fell over a west Cork bóithrín at Beal na mBlath on Tuesday 22 August 1922. Richard Mulcahy succeeded Collins as commander-in-chief of the army, and despite numerous calls for reprisals against republican prisoners held in custody by the more vengeful officers in the Free State army, Mulcahy refused to sanction any mass killings. The ripple effect of the news of Collins' assassination reached Tralee later that evening. Billy Mullins, a senior republican prisoner in Tralee jail, recalled how he heard the news:

> Towards the end of August Captain Danagher, who was in charge of the gaol, walked over to me and asked me to keep all the other prisoners inside for the remainder of the night. He said he feared he might find it hard to control the men in his guardroom and keep

them from coming in to attack us. I asked him what happened. He said Michael Collins was killed in north Cork today. I was sorry to hear of his death. Collins and I were good friends even though we differed very much in our views. Most of the night we could hear the rumpus going on. We were really expecting them to come at us, so we were thankful when morning came.[27]

George Orwell, who served with an Anarchist militia in the Spanish Civil War, a conflict about as far removed ideologically and politically from the Irish Civil War as one can imagine, writing in *Homage to Catalonia* about the ordinary soldier's experience of both that conflict and war in general, noted that it was 'hours of boredom interspersed by moments of sheer terror'. The effects of boredom, combined with a lack of respect for the lethal nature of the weapons the soldiers were dealing with, could lead to pranks or 'play acting' which occasionally had tragic results. The 1st Westerns were responsible for guarding the harbour at the Canal Basin, Tralee, and a seven-man unit was billeted in a house nearby. On 23 August, a sergeant coming to inspect the post was appalled to see one of the soldiers, John Beatty of Lettermore, County Galway, holding a grenade in his hand, from which he had already removed the pin. The NCO shouted at Beatty to throw the grenade in the canal, but as he did so the missile exploded, seriously wounding both Beatty and volunteer Denny Woods from Mount Shannon, County Clare. In the days following the incident both men would die of their wounds.[28]

Soldiers could also be at risk as they handled faulty or poor-quality ordnance. As a precaution, and to be able to respond to attacks like the ones carried out overnight on 21–22 August, patrols travelling to and from Ballymullen barracks began carrying hand grenades in webbing pouches. On the night of 25 August, a four-man patrol en route to Moyderwell were unfortunate enough to have a grenade fall out of its webbing. The patrol commander, Lieutenant Timothy McMahon (25) of Miltown Malbay, dived to the ground to throw the grenade away in case it exploded. The impact of the grenade hitting the ground must have knocked the pin out, and in the subsequent explosion, McMahon and Sergeant Michael Roche (28) from Connolly, County Clare, were killed and the other two men in the patrol were wounded.[29]

On Friday 25 August a large force of Dublin Guards commanded by Fionán Lynch, Minister for Education, who held the rank of general in the Free State army, set out for Kenmare with the intention of both relieving and strengthening the garrison that Tom O'Connor Scarteen had established in south Kerry two weeks earlier. The geographic isolation of the Kenmare military enclave from the rest of the county meant that the troops stationed there could only be contacted and supplied by sea. As the relative deprivation Killarney was experiencing in basic food stuffs due to the cessation of the rail service to Tralee deepened, re-opening the Headford Junction rail line in tandem with a road link to the harbour on the Kenmare river would have represented a huge advance on several fronts.

As the column advanced along the Killarney–Kilgarvan road, it came under fire from republicans at Filadown, near Glenfesk. This brought the ironic comment from Captain Stan Bishop to General Fionán Lynch, TD for the area: 'I believe some of your constituents would like to talk with you.'[30] Reaching a particularly steep rocky cliff face known locally as 'Robbers Den', the intensity of republican

Brigadier Paddy O'Daly, O/C of the Dublin Guards.

General Fionán Lynch of the Dublin Guards.

Captain Matthew McGrath and Captain Brian O'Grady, part of the Free State force that landed at Tarbert.

Fenit Pier on 4 November 1919.

Kerry No. 1 Brigade take over the Staff barracks, Tralee, from the
British army in January 1922.

The workhouse in Listowel after a fire following evacuation by republican forces in July 1922.

Free State troops awaiting billets in Listowel after the march from Ballylongford, August 1922.

Free State troops making arrests in Listowel, August 1922.

Free State troops packing sandbags outside Listowel, August 1922.

Free State troops testing Lewis guns in Listowel, August 1922.

Republicans outside the RIC barracks at Ballybunion before they destroyed it, July 1922.

Free State soldiers in Ballybunion in front of a locomotive.

Train wrecked by republicans near Ardfert on 18 January 1923.

Engine derailed by republicans at Ballybunion, January 1923.

KERRY PEOPLE

XX   Registered at the G.P.O. as a Newspaper   **TRALEE, SATURDAY, AUGUST 5, 1922.**   PRI

OFFICIAL REPORT.

The Landing at Fenit.

Of the Free State Troops.

The March on Tralee.

Engagement at the Spa.

Fights at Christian Bros. and Pembroke Street.

Fierce Struggle in Boherbee.

The Entry to the Town.

Ballymullen and Police

ITEMS OF THE FIGHT

FRIDAY.

Two railway bridges, so far as is known, have been destroyed, one at Ballycarthy, and the other at Bally-seedy.

The people of the town, under all the circumstances, kept very cool heads during the trying times of Wednesday.

The casualties among the Republican forces are not known. Various estimates are given, but of course, they cannot be taken even as approximately correct.

The Boherbee-Moyderwell fight was a very stiff one. A large motor lorry was drawn across the entrance to Moyderwell, and on and 'round this the barricade was erected.

The fighting here and at the railway gates at Pembroke St., was the fiercest of the struggle.

No trains left and entered Tralee on Wednesday evening; and of course no mails were delivered on Thursday.

Mails, however, are being delivered to d.v.

AMNESTY AND PARDON

GOVERNMENT'S OFFER TO ALL IN ARMS AGAINST THE STATE

TO STOP THE BLOODSHED

The following Proclamation, offering an amnesty to all those in arms against the State who deliver up the weapons in their possession and cease to take part in armed opposition to the Government, on or before October 15, was issued last night by the Government of Saorstat Eireann:

TO ALL WHOM IT MAY CONCERN.

1. Certain persons arrayed in arms against the State, in an attempt to defeat by force the will of the people, have created a state of armed rebellion and insurrection, in the course of which the lives of citizens and soldiers of the State have been taken, their liberty violated and vast quantities of public and private property plundered and destroyed.

2. The Government, with the sanction of Dail Eireann, has charged the National Forces with the task of suppressing the rebellion, of restoring peace and order and the rule of law, and of securing to the citizens full protection of life, liberty and property; and for the better carrying out of this task the Government and Dail Eireann have sanctioned and approved the exercise by or under the authority of the Army Council of certain powers, including power to set up Military Courts for enquiring into charges against persons alleged to have participated in the said rebellion and the acts aforesaid, and to inflict punishment in respect of such charges, where proved.

3. The Government, however, knows that many such persons have been forced to participate in such actions against their will and better judgment, while others have come to realise that they have, in truth, put their hands to the ruin of their motherland; and the Government, moved by the hope of restoring peace without further bloodshed and loss, has, therefore, decided that an opportunity be offered even now to those who are willing to throw in their lot with the majority of their countrymen to withdraw from this rebellion with immunity for themselves.

KNOW THEN AND IT IS HEREBY ANNOUNCED AND PROCLAIMED AS FOLLOWS:—

(I) Every person who is engaged in such insurrection and rebellion against the State as aforesaid, or in such armed opposition to National Forces as aforesaid, or who has been guilty of any offence against the State, directly arising out of such insurrection, rebellion and armed opposition as aforesaid, and who, on or before the 15th day of October, 1922, voluntarily delivers into the possession of the National Forces all fire-arms, arms, weapons, bombs, ammunition and explosives and all public and private property, now unlawfully in his possession, and quits all lands or buildings unlawfully occupied by him, and who, on or before the 15th day of October, 1922, voluntarily ceases to take part in, or aid or abet such insurrection, rebellion or armed opposition; shall be permitted to return unmolested to his house; and to every such person we hereby offer, assure and proclaim a full amnesty and pardon for all such insurrection, riot, rebellion, and opposition and offences as aforesaid.

(II) Every such person may deliver any such firearms, arms, weapons, ammunition, explosives and bombs, and any such public and private property as aforesaid, to the Officer Commanding the nearest Military position, or station, or to any such person as shall be nominated by him.

Published at Dublin this 3rd day of October, 1922.

SIGNED ON BEHALF OF THE GOVERNMENT OF SAORSTAT EIREANN,

Contemporary newspaper reports on the developments in the Civil War in Kerry. *Left*: The report of the amnesty offer from the *Freeman's Journal*, 5 October 1922.

rifle fire increased, wounding eight of the soldiers in the Free State convoy. Even though the convoy included an 18-pounder in its arsenal, the steep cliffs rendered it useless and as this, combined with the descending darkness, favoured the riflemen, Lynch and his colleagues decided that retreat was the best option, as to drive any further into the ambush would lead to the engulfment of the entire government force. Army sources later issued a statement to the effect that in a follow-up search of the area the next day they discovered twenty bodies.[31] This was purely a face-saving exercise, giving the impression that they had inflicted heavy casualties on the enemy prior to retreating. In reality, the republican tradition honoured the dead with highly symbolic militaristic funeral rituals; dead bodies would not have been abandoned where they fell. In a further press release (presumably focusing on the same incident) in early September, the authorities announced that Erskine Childers had been wounded, possibly killed, in an engagement between Killarney and Kenmare. The report was without foundation and was essentially another propaganda exercise.

At 3 a.m. on Sunday 27 August, twenty-eight-year-old Seán Moriarty was taken from his home at Walpole Lane, Tralee, by armed men who wore trench coats, green pants and green leggings, and who, according to his mother (in evidence given to a later inquiry) accused him of being at the barracks, a charge he vociferously denied.[32] At the same time James Healy, a former British soldier, was roused from his bed at No. 11 Cowen's Lane and joined Moriarty on a walk to a field in Ballonagh, where both men were shot several times and left for dead. Moriarty died of his wounds, but Healy survived his injuries by lying as still as possible and by pretending to be dead until the assassins had left the scene.

It is unclear why these two men were singled out as suitable candidates for the first *ad hoc* execution in Kerry. It is possible that the military authorities obtained information to the effect that Moriarty and Healy had some involvement with the Ballymullen barracks grenade attack of a few evenings earlier. The reality is that we will probably never know the real reason for their selection.

According to Billy Mullins, the 'murder gang' personnel were scattered when it turned out one of the men survived the shooting. Mullins himself had been stalked by a similar 'unit'. Captain James McNamara, a senior military intelligence officer at Ballymullen barracks had given Mullins a fortnight's parole to see his father, who was gravely ill. As he left the office Mullins did not like the looks he got from some of the officers seated in the ante-room. Mullins did not sleep at home, staying at a neighbour's house across the road. He noted:

> About 4 a.m. people in the house called me to their front room. I could see some Free State soldiers hammering my door with the butts of their rifles. I saw my sister at the window upstairs asking what did they want. They wanted to see me. She said 'what a fool he would be, to allow your murder gang to capture him'. Next morning I called to the barracks. 'Your murder gang called to my house at 4 a.m. [Mullins told McNamara]. I came up to tell you that if anything happens to me while out on parole, your number is up. You'll definitely get it.' He denied any knowledge of a 'murder gang'.[33]

On Monday 28 August, a column of 1st Westerns under the command of Captain James Burke (aged twenty-seven) of

Dunmanway, County Cork, left Killorglin on a march to Tralee, in what was probably the first change of guard since the Killorglin garrison was established on 17 August. The column came under fire at Steelroe, about two miles outside Killorglin. The ambush party, four men armed with rifles and a Lewis gun, was too small to successfully challenge the column, reputedly consisting of almost 100 men, and was overwhelmed and captured. The report noted that two of the prisoners were from Cork and there was particular satisfaction in capturing a Lewis gun. The column came under fire for a second time at Castlemaine, in a gun battle that lasted for two and a half hours. Captain Burke, who was on horseback and at the head of the column, was shot dead near Castlemaine Railway Bridge. The National Army claimed to have killed six and wounded seventeen Irregulars during this engagement, which was the principal ambush in what was a hard march to Tralee. The report contained no details of the column's own casualties, apart from Burke's death; and one should be extremely sceptical of the estimates of republican casualties provided by the army.

Further, smaller attacks occurred about a half mile on the Tralee side of Castlemaine (in what might be described as Humphrey Murphy's own backyard). One happened near Quills Cross, which lasted about a quarter of an hour, and was abandoned as darkness fell. The final assault, which resulted in the death of Volunteer Connors of Ennistymon, County Clare, occurred around midnight, as the column entered Ballyseedy Wood on the final approaches to Tralee.[34] The multiple ambushes on the column indicate a co-ordinated campaign of harassment carried out by local republicans; operations on this scale were rare.

Two soldiers on sentry duty at a checkpoint at the top of High Street, Killarney, at 9.30 p.m. the same evening had a grenade thrown at them. No one was hurt, but a civilian had a narrow escape. The only casualties were two cows belonging to Mr Michael Cronin, who were injured as they grazed in a field on Rock Road. Troops arrested a young fellow named O'Connor, who admitted throwing the bomb.

The hand grenade was a popular weapon of attack in Tralee also. On Friday 25 August, at 9 p.m., a grenade was thrown at troops guarding the GPO on Edward Street from the upstairs window of the Christian Brothers' school across the street. The grenade failed to explode. A sentry rushed upstairs inside the GPO and fired a volley of shots into the open upstairs window of the school.[35]

As darkness fell on Monday 28 August, a grenade was thrown from under the archway at Gas Terrace, Tralee, at a car carrying an army patrol. The grenade exploded but there were no injuries. The troops in the car fired into the alley but no one was injured either by the shots or the grenade explosion.[36]

The relative inexperience of O'Connor, the republican volunteer who carried out the attack in Killarney, reflects the hit-and-miss approach of many IRA assaults on the Free State army carried out in urban areas, which suggests a desire to get the action over as quickly as possible, so as to avoid being killed, wounded or captured once the enemy returned fire. On other occasions, such as shots being fired at GS&WR employees repairing the line at Ballyseedy, on Wednesday 30 August, or rifle fire that wounded four soldiers on board a train at the deer park as they returned to Killarney having provided a work crew-cum-military escort at the same repair site, the republican attacks were primarily carried out as a deterrent. The Kerry rail network was constantly under attack. Each time the line was damaged follow-up repairs restored the rails to a serviceable working order, only for it to be destroyed again. The long-term effect of the disruption of the rail service was actually more acutely felt by the civilian population than the military.

In late August the cable stations in Valentia and Waterville were attacked by republicans, who arrived by boat and destroyed the broadcasting equipment and damaged the cables. The Valentia station was still out of order as late as 5 September, according to a report from the Press Association, dated 6 September 1922.[37] However, around the time of this destruction, General Eoin O'Duffy, O/C South Western military district, referring to the situation in Kerry, noted: 'I am confident in a fortnight we will have the county pretty well cleared.'[38] These comments were made with O'Duffy's usual theatrical flourish with a view to bringing his tenure in the army – and his military legacy – to a close, as by the end of August he had already decided to accept the post of Commissioner of the Garda Síochána, the state's new police force, effective from 11 September 1922. General W.R.E. Murphy, O'Duffy's adjutant, was to be appointed his successor.

The republican view of the Kerry campaign was diametrically opposed to the perspective outlined by O'Duffy. By late August they had regained the initiative after being thrown off balance by the surprise coastal landings at the beginning of the month. In the interim the county's rail network was virtually shut down. While it was true that the enemy held Kerry's principal towns, in many respects they were isolated outposts staffed by 'outsiders' who had little or no local knowledge of Kerry's topography and terrain. The exception was the O'Connor garrison in Kenmare/south Kerry, which was marginalised and cut off from the remainder of Kerry command.

During August the Free State army had twenty-two soldiers killed and about fifty wounded, including Brigadier O'Daly and Colonel McGuinness, which was the equivalent of the total RIC death toll during the Kerry IRA campaign during the War of Independence between January to mid July 1921. Since the beginning of August – and the 'invasion' of Kerry – the Provisional Government had lost their two principal leaders, Arthur Griffith and Michael Collins. Many in positions of command in the Kerry IRA would have seen Collins' successors, Mulcahy, O'Higgins and Cosgrave, as lacking the stomach to face down the republicans militarily. The republicans had everything to gain by continuing to fight. The Republic was still there to be won, at least in Munster.

CHAPTER 4

REPUBLICAN GAINS FROM KENMARE TO TARBERT

On Friday 1 September, Colonel Hogan, 1st Western Division, commandeered some forty horses and carts, got them loaded with supplies in Tralee, and sent a convoy of troops to guard them by road as far as Farranfore. Three miles from Tralee, at Ballymacthomas, fire was opened on the convoy. The troops returned fire and there were no injuries. At Farranfore the supplies were guarded overnight, and next morning they were sent to Killarney by train.[1] This was the first humanitarian food convoy organised by the National Army in Kerry. The gesture was as much about satisfying 'hearts and minds' across Kerry, as it was about filling mouths and stomachs in Killarney.

John Joe Sheehy had a permanent force of three columns (about seventy to seventy-five men) stationed in the Ballymacthomas area, at Ashill, the point where both the Tralee–Killarney road and rail lines converged, providing an ideal ambush location from which to harass the three daily military convoys that travelled each way between Tralee and Killarney.[2] From a republican perspective any convoy guarded by troops was seen as a legitimate military target, in the same vein that Red Cross medical orderlies, who wore army uniforms but were unarmed, were seen as an essential part of the enemy war effort.

The practice of ambushing the 'military component' escorting food supplies primarily destined for civilian use, reputedly caused dissent within republican ranks. According to an article in the *Freeman's Journal* entitled 'Mutiny among the Irregulars':

> [There was] controversy arising out of the recent ambush of a food convoy between Tralee and Killarney at Farranfore. Tom McEllistrim was opposed to the attack, whereas Humphrey Murphy favoured the tactic. At Farmer's Bridge, in an argument over the tactic, blows were exchanged and shots fired. The majority sided with the McEllistrim view. Only a hard core, forty, backed Murphy, who said, 'he could hold Tralee for three years against any force any Irish Government would send against him'.[3]

There is no independent source of verification of this report, other than newspaper coverage, so we have no way of knowing how much of the detail, if any, is factual and how much is spin issued by army sources. Tom McEllistrim was independent-minded and had a genuine concern for the way the conflict was impacting on the civilian population, as well as the damage intercepting food convoys was causing to the perception of the republican campaign in wider public opinion across Kerry. In reality, each IRA column was an intensely local unit and more often than not its cohesion was reinforced by a personal loyalty to a charismatic leader. In this context, McEllistrim's men would have supported his stance. In practical terms he could have decided not to participate in similar actions in the future. Realistically the differences of opinion could be more accurately described as dissent rather than mutiny within the ranks. As O/C Kerry No. 1 Brigade, Humphrey Murphy was senior to Tom McEllistrim and took a far more militaristic approach to confronting the enemy. This was evidenced when, at a later stage in the conflict, Murphy declared that any vehicle bearing 'Red Cross' markings would be regarded as an armoured car rather than an ambulance and would be treated accordingly by the men in his command.

If there was a difference of opinion within republican ranks on the morality of attacking food convoys primarily aimed at assisting civilians, the crisis of conscience was short-lived, as such attacks continued unabated over the winter and spring of 1922–23. As the sole representatives of the civil power in Kerry, the army had no choice other than to provide armed escorts to ensure safe delivery of supplies in a county where opportunistic criminals commandeered goods and republican columns provisioned their armies by scavenging food from larger farms or robbing items such as bacon or flour etc. from the larger wholesalers in Kerry.

The *Cork Examiner*, in a vociferous editorial, addressing the issue of republican interference with food supplies in Kerry, pulled no punches when it stated:

> The measures being taken in Killarney in connection with the flour supply (pending the appointment of a flour controller, to be chosen by the people) serve to emphasise the fact that an artificial famine has been created by those who have interrupted the ordinary distribution services. One wonders if those responsible

for this temporary hold-up of the people's chief article of food in parts of Kerry are proud of this achievement, or do they believe that they are helping Ireland's cause by inflicting loss and inconvenience on the helpless classes? The people of Kerry have always been recognised as the keenest and cleverest in Ireland, and Killarney, which in the past not only fed its own population, but provided large numbers of tourists with excellent – even luxurious – fare, is now to all intents and purposes to be rationed because a number of individuals have seen fit to put the railways out of gear and to make the roads impassable. What is the meaning of this attack on the people is difficult to understand, but common sense should enable this minority to see that these methods of procedure will neither add to their popularity, nor bring a single convert to their views. The present phase is only a passing one, as ample military measures will certainly be adopted to ensure for the different Kerry towns an ample food supply, and steps in this direction have already been taken in Tralee. It is scarcely likely that Killarney, or any other Kerry centre will admit the right of any section to put them on short rations ... politics may, and do, create differences of opinion, but to cut down a man's breakfast because he does not agree with him ... Even John Bull didn't attempt this. The sad part is, it is old people, sick people, lunatics and growing children who are the ones being most put out by short rations. People will remarkably put up with rationing; but they will not surrender indefinitely to outside interference with their daily bread.[4]

Regardless of press criticism, the republican campaign against the railways continued; during the first week in September, a railway bridge at Kilmorna, near Listowel, was blown up. Telegraph lines were cut and a small bridge between Tralee and Ardfert was destroyed. While all these attacks occurred in remote rural areas, well away from any measures the authorities could take to prevent them, a midnight raid on Killarney station on Wednesday 6 September, aimed at burning the signal cabin, was successfully beaten off as it occurred virtually on the doorstep of the Great Southern Hotel, the National Army's Killarney HQ.

Republican actions also came under severe censure from the Catholic Church. On Sunday 3 September, a letter from Dr O'Sullivan, Bishop of Kerry, condemning the killing of the two unarmed Red Cross soldiers at Innisfallen, was read out by Father Casey, parish priest at Curragheen church. An anti-Treaty leader in the congregation blew a whistle, whereupon the IRA contingent left the church en masse and held a meeting in the church grounds, which criticised Father Casey and challenged his knowledge of politics. The IRA response at Curragheen wasn't unique, as republicans carried out similar protests at churches in Abbeydorney, Ballymacelligott, Clogher and Currow.[5] In extreme cases, the criticism of individual clergymen precipitated more direct action. Father Alexander 'Sandy' O'Sullivan, CC, Milltown, a chaplain in the British army during the First World War and described as a vehement supporter of government action, was shot at on Saturday 2 September as he walked along the Milltown–Castlemaine road. Four shots were fired from near the wall of the Godfrey Estate; Father O'Sullivan jumped over the wall to pursue the assailant, who escaped.[6]

More politically astute republicans such as David 'Dead Eye' Robinson, a cousin of Erskine Childers from County Tipperary, who served as a major in the tank corps in the British army during the First World War, and took part in the republican assaults on Kenmare and Killorglin, was concerned for the safety of clerics such as Father O'Sullivan. The propaganda value of the death of a priest at the hands of the republicans for both the government and pro-government newspapers like the *Freeman's Journal* would be incalculable. In an attempt to defend the action against O'Sullivan, Robinson stated: 'O'Sullivan carries a gun and recently fired at some of our men.'[7] It is not clear if he was referring to the Milltown incident.

On Monday 4 September, at 9.30 a.m., a convoy of three Model Ts, with four men to each car under the command of Captain Billy Foley, left Cahirciveen to travel ten miles to Waterville to pay the wages of the garrison stationed there. Sergeant Donal Daly of Kanturk, the paymaster, travelled in the second car and the convoy treated the journey almost like a social outing, so much so that two of the soldiers in the convoy were dressed in civilian clothes. As the patrol passed over Ohermong Bridge, republican scouts decided this would be a good place to ambush the convoy on its return journey. Jeremiah O'Riordan, O/C Kerry No. 3 Brigade, approved the ambush but didn't participate in or direct operations.

A republican checkpoint was set up at Ohermong Bridge to caution people not to warn Free State authorities in either Cahirciveen or Waterville of the planned attack. Houses near the scene of the ambush were evacuated and some locals were detained to prevent sympathisers passing on information. A force of about forty republicans readied themselves for the attack. The main force of about twenty riflemen, and a Lewis gunner (John 'Gilpin' Griffin, a veteran of the First World War), took up positions on the south bank of the river. Ten men commanded by 'Guy' Golden, who was armed with a Thompson submachine-gun (and who gained combat experience in the US army in the First World War) dug in on the west side of the river. The remainder, about eight men under James 'Jama' O'Connell, aligned themselves on the eastern side of the bridge, near the Portmagee road.

The convoy left Waterville about 6.30 p.m. and when they reached Aghatubrid locals told them of the ambush that awaited them. They were advised to turn back as they were greatly outnumbered. With a sense of bravado came the reply: 'We never ran away from a fight and we're going right through to Cahirciveen.'

As the convoy passed through a wooded area in Aghatubrid, the men in the second car fired a volley on either side of the road in case the ambush party was among the trees, and the vehicles spread out so as to reduce their profile as a target. The cars entered the ambush area about 7 p.m. and all three vehicles were hit by a fusillade of fire. The soldiers jumped out and sought cover. Jack Kearney was badly wounded and Sergeant Donal Daly sustained a flesh wound. Thige Murphy, the patrol's Lewis gunner, and Captain Foley managed to take cover behind piles of ballast and exchanged fire with the main ambush party for about half an hour. The other eight soldiers took cover near the bridge, but were unable to see any of their attackers and were too exposed to return fire. Foley's priority was to use a lull in the fighting to get Kearney to Cahirciveen, lest he die of his injuries. During a respite in the shooting a republican, Batty Sheehan, moved towards the Free State positions, whereupon Captain Foley jumped on him and took him prisoner.

As darkness started to fall, the main ambush party began to leave the area, but James O'Connell's unit found themselves on the same side of the river as the Free State troops, inadvertently blocking the very route that would allow Foley's patrol to return to their cars and head back to Cahirciveen. Two of the Free State soldiers, Lieutenant Clement Cooper and Sergeant John O'Donoghue, advanced across the field towards O'Connell's unit. In an exchange of fire Cooper was shot dead and O'Donoghue mortally wounded, and the republican commander, James O'Connell, was wounded in the neck by a ricochet bullet. While O'Connell's injuries weren't life-threatening, the sight of their leader bleeding heavily caused anguish for many of the men in his column, most of whom had never been under hostile fire before the action at Ohermong. Sensing his men's fear, O'Connell wanted to calm their anxiety, shouting, 'Sure I'm not dead, I'm alive. What's the panic for?' Brady, a medical student from Caherdaniel who served as the unit's first-aid man, advised O'Connell that more expert treatment was needed and consequently the force retreated from further confrontation. The Free State patrol returned to Leslie's Hotel in Cahirciveen to get medical attention for their wounded. A large body of very angry troops went to Ohermong to search for O'Donoghue's body. While they were away Captain Foley hid Sheehan, his prisoner, lest the returning troops would kill him in reprisal for their two dead comrades. He later allowed Sheehan to slip away.[8]

On the same day as the Ohermong ambush, it emerged that a maritime solution was already in operation to alleviate the acute food shortages caused by the republican disruption of land transport networks in Kerry. A steamer of the Moore and

McCormack Line had sailed for Kerry the previous week with 2,600 tons of grain and flour on board. According to the *Cork Examiner*: 'the company had established a regular sailing between Cork, Kenmare and Cahirciveen, which they intend to maintain. This will be gratifying news to the inhabitants of the county and do much to relieve the hardship of a sorely tried people.' The news did not go unnoticed within republican circles in south Kerry. It seems the republican assault later that week on Saturday 9 September, was initially planned to intercept the cargo carried by the Moore and McCormack vessel, in particular stores of provisions, food and ammunition carried for the benefit of the military billeted in Kenmare.

On 5 September, the 1st Southern Division O/C Liam Deasy, writing to Ernie O'Malley, expressed his satisfaction with the republican campaign in Cork and Kerry:

Generally, the position here is very satisfactory, particularly in the Cork and Kerry brigades. The enemy occupy forty-eight towns: total troops would be approximately 5,330. Practically all posts are supplied with either an armoured car or armoured Lancia. Their total guns are approximately eighteen. Excepting Waterford and west Limerick, the only districts they have visited to date are Killarney and Skibbereen. All the posts are encircled, and constant harassing tactics are carried out. We are developing the town attack, which was almost a complete success in Bantry on 30th, were it not for the death of Brigadier Gibbs Ross and three other officers. The fight started at daybreak, and at 1.30 p.m. eight of the sixteen occupied posts were taken with eighteen prisoners, twenty-five rifles and 3,000 rounds .303. The remaining posts were attacked, and confined to a square in the centre of town – a much simpler task than the outer posts – but the retreat was found necessary through losses. A seven-hour fight in Macroom resulted in enemy casualties – two dead and six wounded. Various other attacks are being carried out daily. The people are generally becoming more favourable; in many instances the FS troops are in the position similar only to that of the British during the late war.[9]

It is unclear if the larger scale of the assault on the Kenmare garrison was prompted by guidelines from Deasy's staff in the 1st Southern Division, as co-operation and co-ordination between adjacent commands in the republican sector was far from streamlined. Indeed this was not just a republican problem. Eoin O'Duffy did not have a very good rapport with Emmett Dalton and as a consequence there was little co-ordination between the two commands. When troops were deployed in early August, Kerry received 940 men, whereas the Cork contingent numbered 1,180 troops. While Cork is a larger county than Kerry, a total area of 7,422 square kilometres (2,600 square miles) compared to Kerry's 5,254 square kilometres (1,600 square miles), the per capita allocation of troops was one soldier per 5.5 square kilometres in Kerry, and one per 6.25 square kilometres in Cork. In practical terms, however, Cork's 240 extra troops gave the county far more manoeuvrability than their Kerry counterparts.

Deasy's letter to O'Malley not only dealt with military operations in Munster, but also with some of the peace moves initiated by the government's military representatives:

The latter are principally the work of FS officers, including [Tom] Ennis and Dalton, through intermediaries, who apparently are dealing with anybody, politician or military man, who is willing to act. As the republican party were in no way responsible for this war, I consider it unfair to put the responsibility for its continuance or ending on them.[10]

The clear tone of the republican animosity towards the peace overtures stemmed from their view that the war was started by the Provisional Government's armed forces when they shelled the Four Courts garrison. Moreover the Provisional Government/pro-Treaty faction had repudiated the electoral pact worked out between Collins and de Valera, where they agreed that a panel of pro- and anti-Treatyites would stand and after the election form a coalition government. On the eve of the 16 June elections (as republicans saw it) the pro-Treaty party chose instead to throw in their lot with 'non panel' candidates, like Labour and the Farmers' Party etc. After the election these candidates held ninety-two seats, creating a republican minority of thirty-six. Had the electoral pact been honoured, panel candidates (ninety-four TDs versus an opposition of thirty-four TDs) would have formed the government.

THE KENMARE OPERATION

The Kenmare operation was the first instance of a town assault during the summer campaign. The Free State garrison had an effective strength of 130 troops on Saturday 9 September, and had only been diminished by the transfer of a substantial part of the troop by sea to Cahirciveen,[11] possibly as a response to both the recent republican attacks on the transatlantic cable stations and increased activity by Kerry No. 3 Brigade as experienced at Ohermong earlier the same week. When the assault occurred, about half of the force had been on overnight manoeuvres in Scarteen townland (where the original O'Connor farm was located) and the districts immediately south-west of Kenmare. They had been hoping to encircle the republicans that Brigadier O'Connor's intelligence network believed were about to sabotage/booby trap his family farm as a prelude to ambushing any patrol sent to investigate the reports of republican activity in the area, which may have been a deliberate ruse to draw troops away from the town.

A local republican scout, awaiting the arrival of the republican assault force, which was to approach the town from the east, observed the O'Connor patrol (about sixty to seventy men) returning home scarcely half an hour before the eighty-seven-man force under the command of John Joe Rice had planned to commence their attack on the town, at 7 a.m. Had the two forces' paths crossed en route to Kenmare that morning, events in the town that Saturday might have taken a very different course; at the very least for the lifespans of the O'Connor brothers.

According to Jeremiah Murphy of Barraduff, who took part in the republican attack, most of the force (about seventy men in all) was drawn from the Loo Bridge (3rd) and Kilgarvan (5th) Battalion areas and was mostly riflemen. In order to give the assault an advantage – it was the first time republicans attempted to overwhelm several well-fortified military outposts simultaneously in an 'urban' area – John Joe Rice sought thirty men proficient in the use of rifle grenades (the 1920s' equivalent of rocket-propelled grenades) from the Ballyvourney Battalion area in County

Cork.[12] In the event only seventeen turned up, but their input proved decisive; the psychological impact of the grenades on the defending garrison was as significant as the physical damage they caused to the buildings that protected them.

About a mile outside Kenmare, the republican force split into three sections. Each group was allocated two local men, who briefed them on the geography of the town and the location and strength of the army positions. The National Bank and some adjacent buildings – the Lansdowne Hotel, the post office and the Carnegie Library – were identified by local intelligence as the important targets. The reconnaissance and the intelligence provided by the Kenmare scouts was poor. They identified the Lansdowne Hotel as an army outpost, even though it was not occupied by the military at all, whereas the workhouse located some distance from the town centre which was used as an army barracks, never came under attack. However, once the garrison heard the sound of gunfire coming from the centre of town, twelve of the troops stationed there abandoned the building along with their weapons and equipment.[13] While the main attack got underway, a maverick force of five men – some wearing 'Free State' uniforms – proceeded to the O'Connor home at No. 5 Main Street, where both Tom O'Connor Scarteen and his younger brother John (aged twenty) were sleeping off the effects of the earlier 'night' patrol. Inconceivably no one saw the need to post armed sentries to control entry to the building, which was effectively the command headquarters in Kenmare.

According to Nora O'Sullivan (aged twelve) and Kathleen Moriarty (aged nineteen), relatives of the family who were both employed as servants in the O'Connor household, John O'Connor was shot twice as he descended the stairwell of the house to see what was causing the commotion at the entrance. His brother, Tom, was dragged from his bed and shot in the head.[14] The republican version of the event, as recalled by Dan 'Ballagh' Keating of Castlemaine, was that Con Looney and 'Sailor' Dan Healy carried out the shooting: 'They [the O'Connors] were called upon to put up their hands, but instead went to draw their guns. So they were shot dead. They [Looney and Healy] had no other option.'[15] If the republicans had shot out of a sense of self defence, it should have been possible to wound the O'Connors in both the hands and legs rendering them immobile and incapable of returning fire. It seems instead that the brothers were regarded as renegades by their former comrades and were summarily executed in a vendetta killing. Throughout the Civil War both sides engaged in reprisal killings almost on a routine tit-for-tat basis.

While the O'Connors lay dying, Jeremiah Murphy's unit was firing on the Carnegie Library, which was garrisoned by sixty troops.[16] The building was well protected by sandbags and steel shutters, and small-arms fire had virtually no impact, so it was decided to use rifle grenades. The troops finally surrendered at 10 a.m.[17] Around 8 a.m. a section was summoned to the railway station, which was being used as the republican command headquarters from where John Joe Rice, O/C Kerry No. 2 Brigade and a native of Kenmare, was directing operations. They were ordered to assist the force attacking the National Bank – an impressive stone building – and the adjacent houses on Main Street, the principal Free State strongpoint in Kenmare. Around the same time several National Army men converged from the neighbouring houses to join the garrison in the National Bank, which was coming under concentrated fire from the houses across the street. The republicans had used 'linking' – tunnelling through several houses/an entire street – to devastating effect. To the defending garrison they seemed to appear out of nowhere, giving the Free State troops the impression that they were under attack from a much larger force than was actually the case.

'It was pitiful,' Kathleen Moriarty recalled, 'to hear these men calling for Scarteen.' She noted that the republicans, 'tunnelled from a shop – Maybury's – down through Meighans and half-a-dozen other houses, and right into the sitting room of our own house. And battered their way through into Murphy's opposite the bank.'[18]

The proximity of the two forces led to some confusion; an incident recorded by Jeremiah Murphy, when his unit broke through a fireplace into an adjoining house, is worth noting: 'When the occupants saw us they thought we were some of their own men and they asked us for ammunition. At first I thought they were our own men, as they were dressed in civilian clothes and I almost gave them some ammunition. The mistake was cleared when they fired through the hole and I got hit by a splinter of a bullet as it ricocheted off a stone.'

Murphy was taken to the adjacent pub to get his wound dressed. In the ten-minute interval while he was away the republicans threw an incendiary bomb into the room where the government troops were concentrated and its occupants surrendered. Among the prisoners taken was the soldier whose shot had wounded Jeremiah Murphy a few moments earlier: 'My pal recognised him, and might have shot him there and then, but I suddenly raised the barrel of his rifle, and the bullet went through the ceiling.'[19]

The incident shows how narrow the line was between life and death in the conflict and more chillingly how quickly individuals on both sides could initiate a reprisal killing. About twenty minutes later the occupants of the National Bank surrendered – apparently one of their Lewis guns had jammed.[20] This paved the way for a republican victory in the town centre.

The supply boat docked on the Kenmare river, guarded by a six-man complement, was trapped by a low tide on the cusp of turning. The republicans were lucky and captured the vessel and its contents, initially the sole purpose of the raid, which turned out to be far more successful than it ought to have been. David 'Dead Eye' Robinson, fighting on the republican side (whose comments have added value, as he was a veteran of the First World War), was in fact appalled by the sloppy intelligence gathering, insufficient numbers and lack of support from brigade headquarters.[21] Clearly an element of luck was on the republican side that day.

The *Freeman's Journal* report of the Kenmare attack mentioned that there was a corresponding attack on the Cahirciveen garrison.[22] However, there is no evidence that Kerry No. 3 Brigade carried out a simultaneous assault on Cahirciveen and it is possible that the strengthening of the size of the force there acted as a deterrent. Neither is there any evidence of a co-ordinated approach between Kerry No. 2 (under John Joe Rice) and Kerry No. 3 (under Jeremiah O'Riordan) Brigades to neutralise a common enemy. The absence of possibly as much as one-third of the Kenmare garrison might have given the republican assault force an edge, but in reality it was the inexperience of the defending troops and the vacuum left in the Free State command structure by Tom

O'Connor's death at the start of the engagement that were crucial factors in the loss of Kenmare.

By 2 p.m. the guns finally fell silent in Kenmare, and the republicans who captured the town found themselves responsible for the welfare of 130 prisoners, including the younger brother of Kevin O'Higgins, the Provisional Government Home Affairs (Justice) Minister. At this stage the republicans don't seem to have been politically astute enough either to see the practical use (as a hostage) or propaganda value of such a 'high profile' captive. Of course at such an early point in the conflict, not least because they were in the throes of victory, even brigade commanders such as John Joe Rice, would only have seen the war strategy in the short and immediate term. Fourteen of the prisoners under their control were wounded, though none of the injuries were life-threatening. Interestingly, *The Irish Times* would record the government's casualties as four dead and nine wounded, despite the fact that only two of the garrison, the O'Connor brothers, were killed in the assault on the town.[23]

Local reaction to the fall of Kenmare was mixed. At one level virtually everyone in the area was shocked and appalled by the double killing of the O'Connor brothers. On the other hand there was a degree of admiration and a sense of local pride towards the republicans as 'one of our own', i.e. locals, for the grit and determination they showed in 'putting it up' to the metropolitan army and forcing them to surrender. Barth Houlihan (my mother's uncle), a butcher from Killorglin, was in Kenmare in the wake of the 9 September assault, buying cattle from local smallholders, as livestock fairs had ceased in Kerry since the start of hostilities. The main topic of conversation in town and country was 'the boring of the holes', the term local people used to describe linking.[24] People were amazed that not only were buildings no protection against a determined enemy, but entire streets, if necessary could be knocked through to obtain the objective.

The capture of such a large number of Free State prisoners placed their would-be jailers in a dilemma. The reality was the republicans had neither a holding centre to incarcerate prisoners, nor rations to feed them. None of the individual units involved in the attack could spare men to guard a prison camp, so it was decided to march the men under armed escort in the direction of Kilgarvan. After a few miles the prisoners were effectively released and told their best option was to return to Killarney. Only about fifteen soldiers did that, arriving in Killarney at 5 p.m. on Sunday, where their accounts of the fall of Kenmare were received with consternation.[25]

The Kenmare victory was not only a huge morale boost for the republican war effort in Kerry, but John Joe Rice also found himself in possession of 110 rifles, 2 Lewis guns, a large quantity of grenades and 20,000 rounds of ammunition, as well as a supply of army uniforms which had never been worn, as the September delivery carried the first supplies to reach Kenmare since 10 August. The Cork brigades wanted a cut of the Kenmare haul, but Rice was adamant he would not part with a single rifle. He did give ammunition, however; Ballyvourney and Cork No. 5 Brigades received 5,000 and 4,000 rounds each, while each of the six battalions in Kerry No. 2 were allocated 2,000 rounds apiece.[26] This was a huge boost for them, as up to that point each man was only given fifteen to twenty rounds per engagement. Now they could contemplate much larger exchanges of fire or, alternatively, a series of small ambushes stretching over a period of months.

The Free State authorities claimed that the Irregulars had been well armed and that the attack was well planned, involving about 500 men in all, a highly inflated figure given that the actual size of the force (eighty-seven) was almost fifty men below the level of the garrison defending Kenmare. The government press coverage focused particularly on the brutal killing of the O'Connor brothers as proof of the Irregulars' ignominy. In fact, many involved on the republican side at Kenmare were saddened, if not angered, by the double killing. Tom McEllistrim, for example, visited the O'Connor home to offer his condolences to the bereaved and next of kin.[27]

Apart from the capture of military materials and equipment, the victory at Kenmare brought much booty in the form of general cargo on board the vessel docked at Kenmare pier. Volunteer Jeremiah Murphy recalls the bonanza the ship provided for the ordinary members of the local battalion, who at the best of times had to scavenge for food and provisions, and often as not led a hand-to-mouth existence. He wrote:

The next day, we rounded up a convoy of horses and carts from Loo Bridge to Clydagh and took them to Kenmare to remove supplies from the ship. Arriving there early in the afternoon we found that another ship, similar to the first, had sailed into the bay and being ignorant of the situation because it had no radio, was also captured. The activity on the pier was like that around a beehive on a sunny day. As fast as the winches could load them, a long line of horse-drawn carts drove away to our haunts. This was just what we needed – a good haul.[28]

However, below-cost selling by republicans in the wider Kenmare area meant that *bona fide* trade/wholesalers could not get orders in the locality. A commercial traveller from Cork city was selling his product, when:

> … the shopkeeper told him he got exactly the same quantity of goods at half price from Kenmare. The traveller, who is not in the whiskey trade, observed what happened when some barrels of that precious liquid arrived in Kenmare. One was immediately tapped and its contents were taken away in buckets. It would have been a matter of little difficulty to retake the town that night in spite of the presence of 500 Irregulars in the town. He arrived at Knocknagree. Two soldiers on bicycles were at the head of a column of National troops. A man fired a shot from a doorway, but the bullet lodged between the handlebars. Troops returned fire but the gunman escaped. Three men were arrested, but the trader noted two women wearing shawls were each able to get away carrying a machine-gun.[29]

The latter part of the account shows the sometimes surreal quality of the conflict in Kerry at the time, but the feature also indicates the invisible hand of the censor, insofar as 500 is the 'official' (i.e. government estimate) strength of the IRA in Kenmare.

A few days after the capture of the town, a wireless message was received in London (presumably broadcast from one of the cable stations down the coast) to the effect that a large government force had recaptured Kenmare.[30] This rumour was without foundation, but it probably grew from two separate, but related, incidents. The republicans left Kenmare for the duration of the O'Connor brothers' funeral and then on Monday 11 September, twenty-five of the troops who had been escorted to Kilgarvan the previous Saturday as prisoners returned to Kenmare (in uniform, but unarmed) where they boarded the SS *Celtic* along with five male and ten female passengers. About two miles downriver republicans opened fire on the vessel, but there were no injuries.[31]

The *Freeman's Journal* carried a report that Erskine Childers had directed the Kenmare operations personally, as he had been seen in the town in the wake of the republican victory.[32] The sighting of the ubiquitous Childers was true, but he only arrived in town after the fall of Kenmare to get 'copy' for an article he wanted to write on the victory for the republican *War News*.[33] It is possible that Childers' visit to Kenmare was related to the Order No. 1, an instruction from the 1st Southern O/C ordering all brigade commanders to compile detailed reports of all military actions, town attacks in particular.[34] By identifying the strengths and weaknesses, successes and failures, of both republican and Free State forces, Deasy and Lynch hoped to create a database to assist republicans in carrying out further successful operations.

By pure coincidence, Saturday 9 September 1922 was also the inaugural sitting of the Third Dáil in Leinster House in Dublin, the first occasion that the TDs and the Provisional Government ministers formally convened since the 16 June general election. Having being deferred on several occasions at Collins' behest, it was primarily the arrival of W.T. Cosgrave as Collins' successor on 25 August that enabled the parliamentarians to be given the right to attend the National Assembly. In reality, Michael Collins had hoped to bring the Civil War to a successful conclusion without having to justify the government's actions on the 'battlefield', or have the executive's actions and policies subject to scrutiny by parliamentarians, before establishing the National Parliament. Even though Collins cited the dangerous political situation and stated the personal safety of individual TDs as his prime concern, this showed an 'undemocratic', even a 'Bonapartist', facet to his political profile.

THE TARBERT OPERATION

Since the beginning of August, the National Army garrison at Tarbert was a major impediment to anti-Treaty forces in both north Kerry and west Limerick. It also allowed the government to cut off crossings on the River Shannon which meant that Limerick or Kerry IRA units could no longer jump in a boat and cross the Shannon to County Clare to avoid military 'sweeps'. The Tarbert garrison consisted of twenty-five men drawn from both the 1st Westerns and local men from Tarbert and Moyvane (then known as Newtown-Sandes).[35] While the local recruits lacked the combat experience of their Clare and Galway counterparts, they possessed local knowledge of both faces and places which greatly increased the intelligence base and the military value of the force.

Michael Colbert of Athea, County Limerick (whose brother Con was executed for his part in the 1916 Rising), began to consult with Con Dee of Tarbert, the local republican column leader, on how best to tackle the Tarbert garrison.[36] Local Cumann na mBan members were given the job of observing the habits and routines of the troops to find a chink in their armour. Each Sunday the force in the barracks was diminished by half to enable the troops to attend mass. This attendance took place in the form of a church parade, where twelve men marched in uniform, but unarmed, from their headquarters to the local church as a unit, leaving the rest of the men to hold the barracks. Republicans decided this provided an ideal opportunity to both overpower the smaller force at the church and in the process enable them to capture arms and ammunition, which were constantly needed to enable the republicans to continue and expand their campaign, from the barracks. It is highly unlikely that the Tarbert initiative, which took place on Sunday 10 September, was part of a county-wide strategy in tandem with the Kenmare operations the previous afternoon. After all it was 5 p.m. on Sunday before the news of the fall of Kenmare reached the Dublin Guards at their headquarters in the Great Southern Hotel in Killarney.

Prior to commencing the operation, the republicans cut the telephone and telegraph lines in the town. When Colbert informed the parish priest, Father Jerry O'Connor, of what was happening, the priest was furious and had to be physically restrained by a member of the congregation as he intended to leave the church and inform the garrison of the fate that was about to befall them. As the twelve soldiers attending mass left the church they were taken prisoner by the republicans, who proceeded to their barracks and called on the occupants to surrender. The remaining troops refused to do so, whereupon the republican force (which numbered fifty men) opened fire on the building. The defenders replied in kind.

As the confrontation dragged out into hours, the republicans commandeered the adjacent building and bored a hole through the wall. Through this they inserted a metal pipe and pumped petrol into the Free State headquarters, then fired incendiary bullets into the building to ignite the fuel. According to Jimmy Collins of Abbeyfeale, County Limerick, who took part in the attack, the IRA had used a similar tactic successfully during an attack on Kilmallock RIC barracks in the War of Independence.[37] The response of Captain Brian O'Grady and Lieutenant Egan inside the outpost, was swift. They used every single pot, pan and container they could find to collect the fuel as it was pumped into the building. Sandbags were ripped open and their contents were spread to protect the timbers, the defenders coming under heavy fire all the while. The republican assault force failed three times to ignite the interior of the Tarbert barracks. In one last attempt, they decided to push a number of embers down the dry fifteen-foot pipe. They then poured fresh supplies of petrol along the metal tube, which caused a massive explosion, ruptured the pipe and created a massive fireball. The garrison, having held out until 10 p.m. on Sunday night, had no option but to surrender, as their supplies of ammunition were exhausted and they could no longer keep the flames at bay. The defenders had two men wounded during the assault. Republican gains involved the seizure of two rifles (the garrison destroyed the remainder) and 100 rounds of ammunition.[38]

Press coverage largely focused on the pluckiness of Tarbert's defending garrison, thanks to the army's effective propaganda machine. Nevertheless, the weekend of 9–10 September 1922, with the republican capture of Kenmare and Tarbert, was a disaster for the Free State army in Kerry and a setback they could have done without. By the same token, these actions were a huge morale boost for the anti-Treaty forces in the county and throughout Munster. The Kenmare raid succeeded against all the odds, with bad reconnaissance, poor intelligence and a small assault force on the republican side. It shows a myopic aspect of the IRA campaign in south Kerry that there was no follow-up attack on the Cahirciveen and Waterville outposts. We know there was plenty of shipping available to transport a force to Kerry No. 3 Brigade area, but the opportunity to neutralise two more garrisons and acquire additional supplies of weapons and ammunition was not pursued. The Tarbert operation succeeded for all the right reasons; good planning and intelligence combined with improvisation and the accumulated knowledge based on previous operations. The defending government garrison also showed far more resourcefulness than their Kenmare counterparts.

While the reversal in Kenmare was a shock, the military authorities had been acutely aware that its geographic isolation from the rest of the Kerry command structure would make it vulnerable to a republican attack. The same could not be said for Tarbert. Colonel Michael Hogan of the 1st Westerns was furious at having his men burnt out of their barracks. On Monday 11 September, he set out from Tralee for Listowel at the head of a flying column of 120 men with the aim of capturing as many republicans as he could. The troops captured three prisoners on the first day. They arrested ten men in Ballybunion the next day. Subsequent sweeps in Finuge, Lixnaw, Tarbert, Ballylongford and Listowel brought in twelve, twelve and fourteen men respectively, including Paddy Landers, O/C Listowel Battalion; Dr Roger O'Connor, Medical Officer and Adjutant, Kerry No. 1 Brigade; Matthew Finucane, District Police Inspector, Listowel; and Paddy Mahony.[39] The success of the sweep indicates Hogan had good intelligence on the Listowel command structure and network of safe houses. The details of Paddy Landers' capture show that luck always played a part in any operation. A lone soldier entered the house where Landers was based. A man of great physical strength, Landers worked as a smith in the foundry workshops of the Lartigue railway in Listowel. He grabbed the soldier, who loaded his rifle, but as he was about to fire the weapon jammed. At this point other soldiers entered the house and captured him.[40]

Hogan commented how most of the prisoners who surrendered offered little resistance, but virtually no weapons or ammunition supplies were seized. Nevertheless, he felt a haul of fifty prisoners was a successful outcome. On 28 September, a fourteen-man column surrendered at Doon, near Tralee, handing over seven rifles, two magazines for a Lewis gun and several revolvers.[41]

CHAPTER 5

KILLORGLIN: ATTACK AND TURNING POINT IN THE CAMPAIGN

On 11 September 1922, the same day that Colonel Michael Hogan began his series of sweeps across north Kerry, General Eoin O'Duffy was appointed Commissioner of the Garda Síochána, the state's new police force. General W.R.E. Murphy, O'Duffy's adjutant, assumed responsibility for the South Western Division, an unwieldy jumble of several counties whose east–west axis stretched from Clifden on the Galway–Mayo border to Millstreet in north Cork, with its north–south boundary extending from Thurles to Listowel. Following the army's arrival in Kerry in early August, the county was divided into three military districts: Kerry Southern Division (O/C Fionán Lynch, TD), Kerry Western Division (O/C Paddy O'Daly, Dublin Guards) and Kerry Northern Division (O/C Michael Hogan, 1st Westerns). By late August, Murphy was already adopting a 'hands on' approach to directing the campaign in the south-west. His proposals included establishing pro-Treaty flying columns as a rapid response force to confront the republicans. Each column of fifty men would be on duty for a week at a time and, using bicycles, would cover ten miles a day, billet themselves in local army posts and take part in sweeps with the local garrison. The corps would be accompanied by a car transporting a Lewis gun and would be preceded by three or four scouts who would ferret out ambush parties. Murphy also proposed establishing wireless (radio) stations, at the very least in command headquarters in Tralee and Killarney, and deploying aircraft for both reconnaissance and offensive operations (using bombs and machine-guns) in support of ground troops.[1]

In a sense the flying column proposed by Murphy was the prototype for the 120-man unit that Hogan used so successfully in north Kerry in the wake of the Tarbert barrack burning. In practical terms Murphy was trying to introduce the technological innovations of the First World War (without the trenches) where mobility and speed could be used to encircle and capture republican columns in a similar manner to those Kitchener had deployed against the Boers in South Africa during the guerrilla phase (1900–1902) of the Boer War.

Like his Cork command counterpart, Emmett Dalton, William Richard English Murphy had a distinguished career in the British army during the First World War. He was born in 1890 in Bannow, County Wexford, and after school enrolled in teacher training college in Dublin, qualifying as a primary school teacher. After a short period teaching he opted to become a schools' inspector. He joined the British army cadet school in 1915 and was seconded to the South Staffordshire Regiment. Serving in Belgium, France and Italy, he was awarded the Military Cross and the Distinguished Service Order (with bar) and by the end of the war had attained the rank of lieutenant-colonel. Though broadly nationalist, Murphy did not throw in his lot with the nascent struggle for independence as he did not want to take up arms against former colleagues in the British army. Returning to a career in education, in the spring of 1922 he was asked by both Fionán Lynch and Gearóid O'Sullivan, the army adjutant-general (who had been his contemporaries in teacher training college) to give classes in military tactics to pro-Treaty War of Independence veterans who were being groomed to provide the officer corps of the new National Army. Many of his would-be cadets resented being lectured to by an ex-British army officer. The fact that he had not fought for independence and was now the recipient of a plum job in the new post-independence army rankled with many IRA veterans. Once hostilities broke out in Dublin in late June 1922, Murphy left teaching to return once again to a military career.[2]

By mid September, as Murphy began to flex his muscles as a full divisional commander, the hidden (and not so hidden) costs of the war in Kerry were becoming clearer. Kerry County Council estimated about £118,000 was outstanding in uncollected rates.[3] In Killarney, most shops now only opened two or three days a week, either because they had no commodities on their shelves, or because local people had little income in a tourist town without tourists. The Bishop of Kerry, Dr Charles O'Sullivan, donated £100 to a relief scheme set up to help the town's poorer and elderly citizens.

All the while republicans continued to disrupt food convoys, as they were a source of much needed supplies for their own columns (and the smallholders who provided them with shelter and accommodation) and the army hadn't the manpower to guard each and every delivery. On Saturday 16 September, a fourteen-cart unescorted convoy en route to Killarney was held up by armed men at Brennan's Glen, near Farranfore, and several tons of supplies were stolen. The army, in an attempt to close the barn door after the proverbial horse had bolted, only managed to locate one or two bags of flour in a follow-up search.

When the military did provide an escort the convoys usually got through, habitually coming under heavy fire at several points en route and often at the cost of a couple of wounded men. Over the course of the war the accumulative effect of convoy escort deaths accounted for a quarter (seventeen out of sixty-nine) of all the lives lost by the military in Kerry.[4]

Occasionally civilian lives were also being lost. At midnight on Sunday 17 September, Patrick Power, a thirty-five-year-old Tralee man was walking along Rock Street when a shot rang out and killed him. The next day, a coroner's inquest returned an open verdict, which was another way of saying no one had a clue why he was killed or who might have killed him.[5] It is an illuminating insight into the jaded sense of 'conflict fatigue' that officialdom had become locked into in Kerry after two months of senseless killings. A few days after Power's death the *Cork Examiner* reported:

[Thomas Lyons] a thirty-year-old taxi driver, and a native of Muckross, Killarney, in the employment of Mr McCall of Camden Quay in Cork was driving some lady patients from the Mercy Hospital in Cork to their homes in Tralee. As he arrived at Ballycarthy Bridge, about two miles from Tralee, a shot rang out, resulting in a serious wound to the head. Fr McDonnell arranged to have the ladies conveyed by pony and trap to Tralee, and had Lyons' body taken by horse and cart to Tralee. Following the attack the car was driven away and has not been seen since.[6]

In some respects this killing allows more speculation as to what might have been the reason for this death, than the open verdict surrounding Power's death. Since the start of the Civil War, Ballycarthy had long been a favoured ambush point for republicans. At the time most taxi drivers wore a 'livery' which could easily be mistaken for a military uniform. Most probably the sniper identified the driver as a senior officer in the Free State army and acted accordingly. It is probable that the passengers were screened behind opaque glass and were thus 'invisible' to the sniper. Had he chosen to spray the vehicle with gunfire no one would have survived the ambush.

Around the middle of September GHQ was considering creating a separate command for Kerry and General Murphy was offered the appointment. It would be a difficult posting, as by this point Kerry was regarded as one of the most problematic areas in the country and a challenging and difficult area to pacify, but Murphy accepted. To all intents and purposes Michael Hogan and Fionán Lynch would be controlling events on the ground. On Murphy's first inspection of Ballymullen barracks, the county's principal military installation, his first impressions were unfavourable: 'Barracks in a filthy condition and defences in a very unsatisfactory condition. A determined attack could have carried the place. 600 men needed – at least 400 more are necessary. The garrison at present is insufficient even for guarding the town. We have no striking force at our disposal.'[7] He found the physical state of the barracks bad for morale and had the entire complex cleaned down and white-washed. A power plant was established and troops were set to work improving the standard of the kitchens and latrines. A hospital was also established along with a concert hall, while training courses in field tactics and musketry were set up.[8]

Murphy did not have a very satisfactory rapport with his Defence Minister, General Richard Mulcahy, who felt that Murphy was at the centre of a clique of ex-British army officers bent on undermining his command. Murphy also had poor relations with Brigadier Paddy O'Daly of the Dublin Guards. The former head of the Squad, O'Daly was a committed IRB man and would have shared similar views to Mulcahy on British ex-servicemen. In contrast, Murphy and Fionán Lynch had a long-standing friendship since their teacher training days, and Murphy also lavishly praised Colonel Michael Hogan of the 1st Westerns. He described Hogan as 'a most gifted leader' and noted that his unit's 'officer corps had the pick of graduates/undergraduates of UCC'.[9] This view suggests a degree of social snobbery on Murphy's part, perhaps.

On Tuesday 19 September, the Killorglin garrison outposts came under fire from republicans, in an engagement that lasted four hours. The Free State soldiers didn't know it at the time, but this barrage was a reconnaissance exercise aimed at evaluating the respective strength of the three military strongpoints in the town in preparation for a much more ambitious assault the republicans were planning to launch on Killorglin the following week. Around the same time as the Killorglin ranging exercise on 19 September, a republican unit in east Kerry carried out a rifle and machine-gun attack on the barracks in Rathmore. This incident was a routine action by the IRA and had no wider military objective. There were no injuries reported in either exchange of fire, but republicans did kill and maim government troops in random attacks. On the same day as the Killorglin and Rathmore attacks, Private Chase, a Limerick man in the 1st Westerns, was on sentry duty at Tralee prison when he was hit in the arm by a rifle grenade. He lost a limb, but survived his injuries.[10]

Tuesday 19 September should have been a memorable day in east Kerry, as that was the day General Murphy had planned to launch a massive sweep in the Ballyvourney area in conjunction with Cork command, reinforcing ground operations with air support. However, the operation was compromised when an operative at GHQ with republican sympathies leaked details of the plan to Ernie O'Malley, who passed on the information to Liam Lynch. Lynch subsequently ordered all republicans based in east Kerry and north Cork to go to ground.[11] However, this did not prevent them from effectively carrying out further attacks. On Wednesday 20 September, a sixty-cart convoy travelling between Tralee and Killarney was fired upon from three different points as it passed through Currans village, while in a second attack at Ballybrack, Sergeant McSweeney and Private Dunphy, both Dublin Guards, were wounded. Around the same time newspaper reports noted the death of an army driver named Magee who died of wounds sustained near Dysert, Castleisland, a few days earlier.[12]

Despite Murphy's high opinion of him, an action by Colonel Michael Hogan on 21 September shows a reckless streak in a man who was still just twenty-two years old. While driving two civilians and John Lyden, an army medic from Galway (who had missed the departure of the Dublin boat from Fenit), to Blennerville to enable them to make a later sailing, as they passed through Blennerville village, Hogan spotted what he believed was a group of Irregulars. He parked his car on the bank of the canal and as he had a pistol, he fired several shots at the republicans, who returned fire. Hogan's car was peppered with bullet holes as a result of the fusillade, possibly from a Thompson submachine-gun, which claimed Lyden's life.[13] Hogan's behaviour was reckless in the extreme and could have cost him not only his own life, but also the lives of his civilian passengers.

Government troops could also be subject to death and injury in routine weapons drill. On Saturday 23 September, Captain Matthew McGrath (aged twenty) from Feakle in County Clare, died in Listowel in what was described as an accidental shooting, though no further details were provided.[14] The next day, Sunday 24 September, Private J. Looney from Ballybrack was shot dead in Killorglin while taking part in the line-out, where troops coming off duty collectively removed the magazines from their rifles. The soldiers would then routinely 'clear the action' i.e. discharge a 'shot', secure in the knowledge that all the weapons were unloaded and contained no ammunition. Unfortunately, one bullet remained in the barrel of one of the rifles and the subsequent shot killed Looney, who had served in Kenmare until the 9 September reverse and was subsequently redeployed to Killorglin. He was tended to by local GP, Doctor Hannigan, who noted death had been immediate.[15]

On Saturday night, 23 September, the coastguard station at

Fenit came under attack from a force that the garrison estimated at between 130 and 150 Irregulars. This seems an incredible figure, as the ability of the republicans to put together a force of this magnitude, with sufficient weapons and ammunition to mount a sustained attack on a fixed position, seems highly unlikely. Moreover, operating in darkness, a force of this magnitude would be more likely to inflict more casualties on itself than on the enemy. According to the Free State troops the assault was suddenly abandoned and speculation was that the republicans had aborted the attack because they feared they would be encircled by government troops.[16] Realistically, however, it seems more likely that the reverses in Kenmare and Tarbert had spooked many of the local garrisons, to the extent that many outposts were terrified by the prospect of an attack. In their state of mind a mouse could cast the shadow of an elephant.

The Irish Times of 23 September devoted a sizeable number of column inches to reporting Kerry's experience of the Civil War since government troops had arrived in the county in early August. The report was an accurate, hard-hitting assessment of the military situation in Kerry up to that point. Under the headline 'The Army's Task in Kerry', the report observed:

Irregular strength of about 2,000 rifles. The three local brigades contribute 1,000 to 1,200, which along with the support of adjoining forces can call upon 1,800 to 2,000 men. These figures are guesswork, as there is not sufficient information … In truth beyond the occupation of some important towns, where even the National Army are pinned to their barracks … and cannot leave in less than columns of 100 men. Even in their barracks they are harassed by sniping, or are subject to even more aggressive attacks, while enemy columns several hundred strong move along the hills in full view and with complete impunity. Arms and supplies reach the Irregulars along the coast without challenge, while peaceful trading ships are attacked on the high sea and relieved of their cargoes, while on land every movement of goods needs armed protection to ensure it reaches its destination safely.

On the other hand, Brigadier O'Daly and Colonel/Commander Hogan have an able staff, and possess several strategic advantages, but need to develop sea power, so that regular sea communication can be established. Troop numbers could be doubled, or tripled … a force of 8,000 men would bring the campaign in Kerry to a successful conclusion sooner. A wireless set should be provided for each post.

The Irish Times didn't pull its punches in an editorial line that was a grudging admission (though not stated) that the Irregulars in Kerry were offering stiff resistance to the government and its army's attempts to pacify the county. Consisting of a force of between 1,000–1,100 men, the National Army was grossly overstretched, even if judged by its strength 'on paper', which of course was drastically reduced by having scores of troops tied down in static positions, such as barracks duties, guarding prisons, etc. All these factors reduced its ability to mount an effective offensive against the republicans, who, being a mobile force, had far fewer constraints on their manpower and could pick and choose when and where to engage the enemy.

Following General W.R.E. Murphy's appointment as the O/C Kerry Command (until his promotion in the army restructuring in December 1922), he constantly lobbied Richard Mulcahy to commit an additional 250 troops to Kerry, which he estimated was a realistic figure that would allow his troops to switch from a largely defensive posture to an offensive capability, and would bring the army's strength to over 1,500 troops. It is highly likely that the *Irish Times'* editorial was penned by the paper's war correspondent, Theodore Kingsmill Moore, with his source being none other than General Murphy. It was a journalistic relationship Mulcahy totally disapproved of in his Kerry subordinate.[17] However, despite their inadequate numbers, small scale – though incremental – captures of republican prisoners by the Free State army were whittling down the size of the 'Irregular' volunteer pool in Kerry during the course of the summer campaign. The republicans were focused on gaining as much ground as possible in the summer as, once October arrived, the colder and wetter climate would make the republican campaign, i.e. 'war out in the open countryside', far more difficult to sustain.

ATTACK ON KILLORGLIN

The ink was hardly dry on the *Irish Times'* 'Kerry Editorial', when the republicans sent an envoy to Killorglin informing the population of an imminent attack on the main military outposts in the town and advising them for their own safety to leave town. This warning occurred either late on the evening of Sunday 24 September or early the following day. Most people heeded the advice. While the republicans were anxious to avoid civilian casualties, a totally – or even partially – evacuated town made their task much easier. It would allow them to use the strategy of 'linking' without interference, a tactic which they had used to such great effect in the Kenmare victory. The fact that the

Killorglin force was about half the size (sixty to seventy men) of the contingent they had overwhelmed in Kenmare made the republicans confident of victory.

Captain Donal Lehane (24), the commanding officer in Killorglin, put his men on 'stand to' in anticipation of an immediate attack and established an additional outpost (three men) to protect the town's railway signalling equipment in case the republicans would attempt to destroy it during the course of the assault. The defending garrison also decided to establish an additional outpost in O'Shea's public house, Langford Street. This would make communication between the command headquarters at Morris's Hotel and the RIC barracks easier. Located midway between the two, the pub outpost gave sweeping views of any possible advance crossing Langford Street and protected a blind spot in the Morris's approaches.

All of Lehane's men were on 'stand to' for two to three days. During this time they came under IRA sniper fire. According to Lieutenant Corry: 'From the hills around us they were able to fire from positions of splendid cover. They never hit any of our men, and we never replied to their fire, which seems to have irritated them.'[18] Evidently both sides were engaging in psychological warfare: the republicans trying to identify the strength of the various garrisons and deplete their ammunition stocks and keep them guessing when the main assault would begin, while the Killorglin garrison understood the tactic and gave nothing away. The republicans also needed to wait until they could marshal their force for the main assault. Consequently many of the defending garrisons were on the verge of exhaustion when the republican attack actually began, at 6 a.m. on Wednesday 27 September.

During the previous night republican sappers had tunnelled down the entire length of Upper Bridge Street and placed a massive landmine on the upper floor of Dodd's, the house next door to Killorglin RIC barracks. A massive explosion shook the building and blew slates from the roof, the force of the blast literally throwing Lieutenant O'Callaghan and some of his men from their beds. They sustained minor injuries, but the building saved them from worse, as it had only been constructed in the late 1890s and was far more robust than most of the older housing stock in Killorglin. The republicans made two additional attempts to destroy the building using landmines, but only managed to demolish Dodd's house. Republicans also entered Denny Con O'Sullivan's public house on the other side of the RIC barracks and bored through the fireplace. As the hole opened troops in the barracks threw grenades through it and claimed to have injured several republicans.[19]

An IRA unit from Cahirciveen, consisting of several riflemen under the leadership of Lewis gunner John 'Gilpin' Griffin, had taken up positions in the upper floors of Stephen's shop, directly across the street from the barracks.[20] In a 'trick' shot Griffin fired a single round, which went down the barrel of the Lewis gun in the barracks and blew the ammunition pan off the weapon, tearing away a part of the gunner's upper lip and a large portion of the gun. According to Free State sources the wounded Lewis gunner stayed at his post for a further seven hours.[21]

While landmines were being used against the Upper Bridge Street outpost, which the republicans had selected as the lynchpin of their assault, the Carnegie and Morris's Hotel were subjected to rifle and machine-gun fire. The Carnegie, a free-standing building, came under fire from a Lewis gun operated by Jer 'Romy' Keating of Cahirciveen on the upper floor of an outbuilding at the back of Griffin's public house, and also from the O'Connor house on Mill Road.[22] It is surprising, given the difficulty of mounting a direct assault on the Carnegie, which had a wide open field in front and a hilly copse on its marshy river flank, that the republicans did not use rifle grenades against this building, a weapon that had been used to great effect in the Kenmare attack. The garrison at Morris's Hotel was protected by surrounding buildings and its machine-gun post in the square tower of Killorglin Protestant Church made a direct assault on the outpost by republicans extremely difficult. The *Cork Examiner* reported on 30 September that republicans had succeeded in setting fire to the roof of the Carnegie, but if the report was accurate, the garrison must have got the blaze under control. The *Examiner* also reported on 3 October that two of the garrison were taken prisoner by the republicans, but provides no details on the location or the circumstances of the arrest.

Prior to commencing the assault, Bertie Scully, who was directing IRA units from the republican command headquarters based in the Railway Hotel, decided that if they had failed to overwhelm the RIC barracks by a given time, a signal would be given to all the other strike forces to abandon the entire Killorglin operation. Scully asked Mary O'Sullivan, a Cumann na mBan activist, if she would be willing to walk through Killorglin carrying an opened umbrella, which would be the pre-arranged 'coded' message to the other units to abandon military operations. O'Sullivan quite reasonably objected to the plan, pointing out that it wouldn't work and that even if she agreed to carry out the trek, she would likely be shot either in crossfire or by a Free State sniper.[23] The surreal vision of a Mary Poppins-like figure, complete with opened umbrella, calmly walking through Killorglin in the middle of a major gun battle beggars belief and approaches high farce.

During any lulls in the fighting the republicans called on the defenders to surrender. The replies varied between 'Never', 'Up Clare' and 'Up the 1st Westerns', indicating a strong sense of local pride in both their unit and county of origin, and a determination to resist that had been lacking among the troops serving in Kenmare. On several occasions when republicans were shot on the street, soldiers rushed out, under fire, and seized the rifles and ammunition. Captain Donal Lehane replied to a request for surrender at one point: 'We'll surrender only when our ammunition is spent.'[24]

Lehane seems to have been an inspiration to his men. On one occasion, during a lull in shooting, he stormed the building across the road from Morris's Hotel and, although he sustained a head wound, he and his men managed to take eight prisoners and neutralise the mill/creamery building on Annadale Road, the main republican threat to his headquarters. At 11 a.m. that day his luck ran out, however, and against the advice of his men, he advanced towards republican positions in Evans's pub across the road from O'Shea's outpost, where he had seen both Lewis and Thompson machine-guns. Lehane was killed in a burst of Thompson submachine-gun fire near O'Shea's pub on Langford Street.[25]

Donal Lehane was the third member of his family to suffer a violent death during the War of Independence–Civil War period. In the series of reprisals following the Rinneen ambush in County Clare, where six RIC men were killed in late September 1920, Lehane's father Dan (60), and his elder brother, Pat (known as 'Pake') were both shot by the security forces on their farm at

Cregg, Lahinch. Pake Lehane's body was never recovered as following the shooting his killers burnt his cottage to the ground, while Dan Lehane died of wounds on 26 September 1920, almost two years to the day before his son would meet his death in Killorglin.

The republican headquarters were directly across the road from the railway signal box where the Free State forces had set up an outpost a few days earlier. The post came under sustained attack throughout the day, but held out against the odds, although claims made by the garrison that they killed at least six Irregulars while defending the post seem to be without substance. The defending garrison also claimed that between six and ten Irregulars lost their lives during the course of the assault on Killorglin, including a leader named Clifford and an officer named Slattery. In fact only two republicans were killed during the assault on Killorglin. Patrick Murphy of Dooks, Glenbeigh, was killed in the action. Their second fatality, Con Looney of Kenmare, was sniped at by Lieutenant Corry, O/C at the Carnegie, to avenge the part he was alleged to have played in the death of the O'Connor brothers in Kenmare. Corry was wounded himself while he fired the shot that killed Looney.

While convalescing in hospital, Lieutenant Corry gave an interesting account of the Killorglin battle to 'Iris an Aram', the 'in house' army newsletter, in which he estimated between 300 and 500 Irregulars were involved. The reason such a large concentration of men was available, he explained, was as a result of General Dalton's sweep of the flying columns in north Cork, which saw contingents from Limerick, Tipperary and Cork head for Killorglin to fight alongside their Kerry counterparts. At least eight machine-guns were used in the attack and much of the ammunition stocks taken at Kenmare were used in Killorglin. Some of the republican commanders were so sure of victory in the early stages of the attack, they amused themselves by playing billiards in the Railway Hotel. During the conflict Fr McGrath, Fr O'Donoghue and Dr Hannigan administered aid (both medical and spiritual) to all parties, both National Army and Irregulars alike.[26]

As dusk fell on Killorglin, fearing the republicans would sabotage the town's electricity generating facility on Mill Road, a handful of troops crawled from their Upper Bridge Street base and set up a guard on the building. Random shooting continued throughout the night. At some point during the course of the evening, Fr James Nolan, parish priest of Killorglin, unbeknownst to either the garrison or the republicans besieging the town, got on his bicycle and cycled in the pouring rain to inform the authorities in Ballymullen barracks, Tralee, that reinforcements were urgently needed to save the Killorglin force from defeat.[27] Incredibly, after eighteen hours of sustained assault, attack and counterattack, the Irregulars had not breached the garrison's defences. There was, of course, a tipping point – namely if ammunition stocks were depleted and the garrison sustained too many wounded, the various outposts could be overwhelmed by attrition.

The first Free State reinforcements, a cycle patrol, was fired on at 4.30 a.m. at Castlemaine in an engagement that lasted an hour, before proceeding to Killorglin. Castlemaine had been chosen by the IRA as the best point to challenge the expected relief force. This patrol was only the vanguard of a much larger force under General W.R.E. Murphy and Colonel Michael Hogan, which took nine hours to travel to Killorglin such was the number of obstacles – trenching, fallen trees, etc. – put in place to delay the progress of any relief force. A mine found on Castlemaine Bridge was defused.[28] The reinforcements, 1st Westerns, included the armoured car *Danny Boy* in the convoy.

Nightfall brought about a general lull in the fighting, but republicans were reluctant to leave their posts lest the government garrison would use the lack of vigilance on their part as a way of advancing and consolidating their positions. Effectively the occupation of the town's electricity generating station by Free State troops was a good example of the opportunism of the defending garrison. Anticipating the assault would resume at first light, many republicans remained in Killorglin overnight. As the government's relief force approached the town early on Thursday 28 September, the republicans offered some resistance initially. However, as the size of the force became apparent, the majority of the republicans evacuated their positions, with the exception of a small unit trapped in buildings between the RIC barracks and Morris's Hotel, who were taken prisoner once the reinforcements entered Killorglin.

Given the intensity and the numbers involved in the fighting, it is surprising that the casualty levels were so low – eleven wounded among the defending garrison and only fifteen on the republican side. This was partly due to the use of 'linking', which radically reduced the risk factor for the assault force. In the days that followed, two of the injured would die of their wounds; Jeremiah Keating of Cahirciveen on the republican side and Denis O'Connor, who was described as a 'local scout' for the National Army. It appears that James Guerin was the only civilian casualty; he was seriously wounded when he was caught in crossfire early on Wednesday morning.

The garrison took eighteen republicans prisoner during the course of the fighting in Killorglin, including John Galvin, whom a Free State officer identified in an interview in the *Cork Examiner* on 3 October as 'the man who killed Captain Burke'. This was referring to an incident that happened at Castlemaine a month earlier when Burke, a close personal friend of Colonel Hogan, O/C 1st Westerns, was shot dead at the head of a column of 1st Westerns en route from Killorglin to Tralee. Under interrogation following his capture, in which Galvin's arm was broken, he admitted that he had fired the shot that killed Burke.[29] As the column escorting the republican prisoners reached Ballyseedy, Galvin's captors took him aside and shot him several times, then threw his body into a ditch. The official version of this event was that the army was attacked by republicans and John Galvin was killed in the ensuing firefight. The deaths of both Con Looney and John Galvin show the willingness of the 1st Westerns to engage in reprisal killings.

The situation in Killorglin had returned to normal by Friday 29 September and the relief force returned to Tralee. Later that evening, four republicans returned to one of the houses in the town to retrieve a Lewis gun hidden in a feather bed. As they made their way out of the house with the weapon, they were spotted by a soldier and challenged. After a gun battle lasting over an hour the republicans surrendered, handing over the Lewis gun, rifles, grenades and ammunition, as well as two parabellums and a colt revolver.[30] The willingness of Killorglin republicans to risk their lives to recover a single weapon shows how valuable a Lewis gun was in a column's arsenal.

General W.R.E. Murphy, writing in his diary about the 1st Western defence of Killorglin, noted: 'These Clare men were undoubtedly born soldiers. It was the finest action which the present war has produced.'[31] Such an accolade from a man who was awarded the Military Cross and a DSO in the First World War was praise indeed. In a letter to Richard Mulcahy, penned in early October, Murphy said: 'I would you like to send a few words of appreciation to the 1st Western garrison of Killorglin. This was the finest show of the war outside Dublin. The 1st Westerns are a fine body of men, cheerful, willing and uncomplaining. They are a credit to any army and I cannot speak highly enough of their officers. Hogan is an excellent officer and is worshipped by his men. They would appreciate very much a message from you.'[32]

Murphy's letter also requested permission to invoke the Emergency Powers legislation passed by the Dáil on the same day as the Killorglin engagement. 'We took at Killorglin,' Murphy wrote, 'a Kerry deserter who had deserted with his rifle and 100 rounds. Under new regulations we have to submit death sentences for sanction to GHQ. May I shoot this man, as he is guilty and was caught by us with a rifle and fifty rounds while fighting with the Irregulars?'[33] Mulcahy did not authorise General Murphy's request for an execution.

BRENNAN'S GLEN AND TRALEE

At 6 p.m. on Wednesday 27 September, as battle still raged in Killorglin, a two-vehicle convoy of Dublin Guards (thirty men) was fired upon as they turned a bend in a densely wooded part of Brennan's Glen, near Farranfore. Two men, Daniel Hannon from Belfast and John Martin from Dundalk, were killed and seven were wounded in the attack, which occurred so quickly the patrol was unable to return fire.[34] When the military authorities released details of the attack, it included the information that an Irregular prisoner, Bertie Murphy, who was in the custody of the patrol at the time, was also wounded, and later died of his injuries. On Friday 29 September, County Coroner, Dr William O'Sullivan, presided over an inquest into the death of Murphy. This was unique not only in the fact that it took place at all, but in the sense of urgency the military authorities devoted to establishing the facts surrounding Murphy's death.

Julia Murphy, the boy's mother, giving evidence at the inquest, said Bertie (17) was her eldest son and she had last seen him alive on 27 September, travelling on the back of an army lorry. Brigadier Paddy O'Daly, O/C the Dublin Guards, giving evidence, emphasised that the ultimate responsibility for her son's death lay at the hands of the Irregulars. 'While sympathising with you, as I sincerely do,' O'Daly said, addressing Murphy's mother, 'I cannot help reminding others that two other men lost their lives in the attack which leaves three women bereaved, two mothers and a wife … thinking at present that their sons and husband are alive in Kerry.'[35]

In reality, Bertie Murphy was in military custody when the Brennan's Glen ambush occurred, having been arrested in the Brennan's Glen/Farranfore area earlier on 27 September. He was in one of the basement cells in the Great Southern Hotel, Killarney, the Dublin Guards' HQ at the time of the ambush. When news of the attack reached Killarney, it was assumed that Murphy, a native of the area where the attack occurred, would know who was involved. Following a brutal interrogation during which he revealed no information, Bertie Murphy was shot dead.

On Friday night, 29 September, republicans set fire to the Lock House at the entrance to the Tralee canal and blew up the lock gates. The next day a barge carrying fifty tons of maize was sunk near the entrance to ensure the waterway could no longer be used for either military or commercial traffic. In the process another vital lifeline in the county's transport infrastructure was taken out of use. A notice on board the sunken vessel warned of dire consequences for anybody who attempted to remove the craft from the canal. Around the same time as the canal post was destroyed, a group of off-duty soldiers from the Dublin Guards were talking outside the courthouse in Rathmore. Republicans opened fire with a Lewis gun, killing Sergeant Noonan and wounding four others.

The week following the *Irish Times*' feature on Kerry (23–30 September) had been an eventful week for both belligerents in a campaign that from the perspective of both sides was far from a successful conclusion to the summer campaign.

With the onset of the winter and its unfavourable weather conditions, from mid October onwards republican activity in Kerry was reduced considerably. As late as 21 October 1922, Free State forces stationed in Kerry had only increased by 179 men – from 940 to 1,119 troops (2 August/21 October), in spite of persistent lobbying by General Murphy.[36] Mulcahy gave additional manpower to Murphy's command during November (raising levels to 92 officers and 1,440 men[37]) further increasing the force to 123 officers and 2,463 men by early December.[38] Had these additional forces been committed during August/September, the government forces summer campaign in Kerry might have fared much better and delivered more concrete objectives.

CHAPTER 6

CONCLUSION

The coastal landings in Cork and Kerry in early August 1922 were an inspirational manoeuvre by the government's military planners. They were expected to shorten the war on the ground and fast-forward the demise of republican armed resistance to the Provisional Government. After a short summer campaign, GHQ in Dublin anticipated that with a bit of luck the Munster Republic would wilt in the face of superior numbers of men and equipment, and be on the verge of collapse by mid to late September. The Kerry landings were a tremendous success, taking the republicans totally by surprise and – with the exception of Tralee – the force faced little opposition and sustained few casualties. In little more than a week, 940 government troops had established a nucleus in Tralee and coastal enclaves on the Shannon (Tarbert) and Kenmare rivers. However, once the task forces expanded across the county, their shortcomings were evident. What was sufficient to secure a beachhead was totally inadequate when stretched over a county of over 1,800 square miles, much of it difficult mountainous terrain with poor roads and long fragmented peninsulas.

Once they recovered from initial shock of the landings, Kerry No. 1 and Kerry No. 2 IRA Brigades mounted an effective counterattack, rendering the county's rail network inoperable within a week. The bulk of the government troops operating in Kerry were from outside the county and had no local knowledge. For the republicans this was their home, territory they knew intimately and had used effectively in the war against the British in 1920–21. Added to these advantages, many of the Free State officers in Kerry were poorly trained and most of their troops inadequately grounded in waging conventional warfare and in the case of the Dublin Guards campaigning in a rural area.

The best way of assessing the IRA campaign in Kerry during the summer of 1922 is to compare their activity levels to the conflict the republicans waged nationally in the Civil War up to that point. A comparison of Kerry republicans' actions with their War of Independence campaign is also useful. From the bombardment of the Four Courts on 28 June to 31 July 1922 prior to the commencement of the Kerry campaign, Free State forces had 59 troops killed and 160 wounded nationwide.[1] By mid to late September the casualties had increased to 185 killed and 674 wounded.[2] The Kerry figures, 35 killed 100 wounded, represents a high proportion of the national total for a single county. The corresponding death toll for the republicans in Kerry for the same interval was nine, four of which were reprisal killings carried out by the Dublin Guards and the 1st Westerns.

Comparing the army's death toll for August–September 1922 with the number of police killed by the IRA in Kerry during the 1920–1921 period is illuminating. During 1920 thirteen RIC men were killed in Kerry, while a further twenty-three policemen lost their lives up to the calling of the Truce on 11 July 1921.[3] The Free State army death toll for the month of August 1922 was twenty-two, while thirteen died during September, which contradicts the popular view that Kerry republicans had no stomach for the Civil War. The death toll for the first two months of the Civil War indicates that the republicans waged a far bloodier campaign against the Provisional Government forces, comparatively speaking, than that fought against the British during the War of Independence. If the IRA death toll during the first two months of the conflict is accurate (nine killed, though I suspect it could be an under-estimation), it would represent a lot lower death toll at the hands of the Free State (up to that point) than occurred in Kerry under the British occupation, when thirteen Volunteers were killed in 1920, with a further twenty-seven deaths between January and July 1921.[4]

If one shifts the prism slightly, by conventional military terms the Irish Civil War in general was a low intensity conflict with sporadic outbursts and very low casualties. In the First World War, a battalion 'going over the top' on the Somme or Passchendale, for example, could lose thirty-five dead and 100 wounded within five minutes of leaving the trenches, and these casualties would be considered low. Finland, a small, recently independent country with a population similar to Ireland, fought a four-month Civil War in 1918, which cost over 30,000 lives. The Irish conflict by comparison, lasted six months longer than the Finnish Civil War and probably claimed less than ten per cent of the Finnish death toll.

The assault on Killorglin on 27 September 1922, represented the high water mark for the republican offensive in Kerry, in terms of the time taken to plan the attack, the amount of weapons available and the numbers of men available to attack the garrison on the south-western boundary of the Free State's 'safe' enclave in Kerry. Ironically, the defence of the town became an epic victory in Free State army mythology. An action where two Irregulars were killed and fifteen wounded was, within a week, transformed by propaganda into a battle that inflicted fifty-one dead and ninety wounded on the force assaulting Killorglin.[5]

Town attacks, such as the one carried out in Killorglin, were not driven by a desire by republicans to capture or hold centres of population in Kerry. This strategic shift would have been counter-productive in both the short and long term, tying down republican units and throwing down the gauntlet to the Free State forces to recapture the town. In reality the principal objective of such an attack was to obtain weapons and ammunition held by the garrison, and in the process remove the troops, restoring the rural hinterland 'protected' by the ousted garrison to republican control.

Had the Killorglin action been successful, which represented all the capital – both in terms of weapons and propaganda – the republicans had won at Kenmare, a front line might have developed along the River Laune, extending across the Killarney lakes and into the mountainous areas of east Kerry, giving anti-Treaty forces de facto control over the Iveragh peninsula, not unlike the thirteenth-century division of the county between the Anglo-Norman shire of Kerry and the mountainous Gaelic territory of Desmond. In a domino effect republicans might also have advanced on Castlemaine, using it as a precursor to sealing off the Dingle peninsula, via the Camp road to Castlegregory and linking up with Paddy Cahill's considerable force on Slieve Mish mountain.

Even by early October government troops had made few inroads into the Dingle peninsula, largely because of low activity levels by republicans. In order to hermetically seal off peninsular Kerry, anti-Treaty units would have had to confront and remove the pro-Treaty forces still in place in Cahirciveen, Waterville and Valentia Island. Had Kerry IRA units reached this position by the beginning of October, the republicans would have regarded their summer campaign as having reached a highly successful outcome. In north/central Kerry, however, government troops were increasingly consolidating their control over territories that were marginally and irrevocably being lost to the republican forces in Kerry.

Wednesday 27 September saw the Defence and Justice Ministers, Richard Mulcahy and Kevin O'Higgins, introduce emergency legislation before the Dáil. The Emergency Powers Bill was in effect an admission that, militarily, the government's army was proving inadequate to deal with the resistance it faced in various areas of the country, such as Kerry, where republicans had reverted back to a guerrilla campaign akin to that waged against the British during the War of Independence. For Mulcahy, as Defence Minister, it was also an attempt (largely unsuccessful) to reassert central government control and prevent the commission of ad hoc executions and reprisal killings at local level. The legislation gave the government wide powers of execution for a whole range of offences, including possession of a weapon, ammunition and explosives, which were all designated as capital offences punishable by death. The Emergency Powers Act, carried by forty-eight votes to eighteen (the Labour Party opposed the terms vigorously) allowed a two-week amnesty, extending from 3–12 October, during which time individual republicans could hand over the offensive items proscribed by the legislation.[6]

The Free State Executive Council, largely at Cosgrave's behest, persuaded the Church to endorse the Emergency Powers' legislation. In a Pastoral Letter issued on 10 October 1922, the Catholic hierarchy urged Irregulars 'to take advantage of the Government's offer … and make peace in our country'. The bishops determined it was a matter of divine law, 'that the only legitimate authority was the Provisional Government. There is no other government, and cannot be.' In specific terms, it stated that the warfare carried out by the Irregulars was without moral sanction; therefore the killing of a national soldier in the course of his duty was murder before God. In conclusion the letter stated that any Irregular contravening the Pastoral's moral guidance would not be absolved in Confession, and would not be allowed to receive Holy Communion. In a high-risk conflict situation, where a republican (in most cases, a devout Catholic) risked his life for his political beliefs and principles, to be refused the sacraments was literally a fate worse than death.

It is unclear how seriously the average IRA activist took the death threat implicit in the terms of the new Act. In reality it would be nearly four months (20 January 1923) before the legal powers conferred by the 27 September Act were used in Kerry. In the interim, however, individual officers carried out ad hoc reprisal killings in 'the heat of the moment' if one of their own unit was killed.

Two crucial actions perpetrated by civilians had a huge

bearing in determining the course of the summer campaign in Kerry. Firstly, the decision by employees of Tralee Harbour Commissioners to disconnect the cable on the mine on Fenit pier – for purely apolitical motives (to save their own jobs) – had a profound effect on the campaign of both belligerents. Had the landmine exploded, the result would have been a catastrophe for the Dublin Guards' task force, as the troops could not have left the pier and the ship could not have left the port, due to adverse tidal conditions. At the very least the troops would have had to undertake a Gallipoli-type landing without either their armoured car or field gun. In the worst case scenario from the government's point of view, Kerry IRA might have taken all 450 troops prisoner and captured all their equipment. The second action, a partisan one by the parish priest of Killorglin – at the other end of the summer – enabled a relief force to rescue the pro-Treaty garrison based in the town. Without the relief force, the Killorglin garrison would have eventually been overwhelmed both by a combination of depleted ammunition stocks and the sheer strength of numbers of the republican assault force. These two actions changed the course of the campaign in Kerry, denying the republicans the chance to take a firm hold on the county and allowing the Free State to maintain a presence in a crucial part of the republican's heartland.

Appendices

1. National Army, killed or died of wounds

Name	Date of Death	Place	Birth Place
Burke, James (Capt)	28/08/22	Castlemaine	Dunmanway, Cork
Byrne, Edward (Pte)	02/08/22	Spa, Tralee	Pimlico, Dublin
Carson, William (Cpl)	02/08/22	Pembroke St, Tralee	Belfast
Connors, — (Pte)	28/08/22	Ballyseedy woods	Ennistymon, Clare
Cooper, Clement (Lt)	04/09/22	Cahirciveen	Kilcummin, Kerry
Daly, Michael (Sgt)	23/08/22	Castleisland	Dublin
Farrell, Michael (Cpl)	02/08/22	Pembroke St, Tralee	James' St, Dublin
Fitzgerald, Cecil +	17/08/22	Killarney lakes	Gort, Galway
Galworthy, John (Pte)	24/08/22	Ballymullen barracks	Innisboffin, Galway
Gillespie, Fred (Sgt)	02/08/22	Pembroke St, Tralee	N.C. Road, Dublin
Hannon, Daniel (Pte)	27/09/22	Farranfore	Belfast

Note: Where + appears beside a name it denotes a member of the Army Service Red Cross

N.A. stands for details not available

Harding, Patrick +	02/08/22	Pembroke St, Tralee	James' St, Dublin
Houlihan, Brian (Capt)	05/08/22	Castleisland	Kenmare, Kerry
Kavanagh, Tom (Pte)	24/08/22	Kilcummin	N.C. Road, Dublin
Kenny, John (Pte)	02/08/22	Pembroke St, Tralee	Coombe St, Dublin
Larkin, Thomas (Pte)	02/08/22	Castle St, Tralee	Howth, Dublin
Lehane, Donal (Capt)	27/09/22	Killorglin	Lahinch, Clare
Lyden, John +	21/09/22	Blennerville, Tralee	Co. Galway
Lydon, John (Sgt)	18/08/22	Spa, Tralee	James' St, Tralee
Magee, Michael	11/09/22	Castleisland	Dublin
Martin, John (Pte)	27/09/22	Farranfore	Dundalk, Louth
Murphy, John (Pte)	20/09/22	N.A.	N.A.
Murphy, Will (Sgt)	16/09/22	N.A.	N.A.
Noonan, Edward (Sgt)	28/08/22	Rathmore	Dublin
O'Connor, Denis (Pte)	29/09/22	Killorglin	Kerry
O'Connor, James (Pte)	02/08/22	Pembroke St, Tralee	Summerhill, Dublin
O'Connor, John (Capt)	09/09/22	Kenmare	Kenmare
O'Connor, Tom (Brig)	09/09/22	Kenmare	Kenmare
O'Donoghue, John	04/09/22	Cahirciveen	Kerry
O'Meara, John +	17/08/22	Killarney lakes	Galway city
Quane, John (Pte)	12/08/22	Bedford, Listowel	Meelick, Clare
Quinn, Patrick (Pte)	02/08/22	Kilfenora, Tralee	Poolbeg St, Dublin

O'Reilly, Patrick (Pte)	02/08/22	Pembroke St, Tralee	Gardiner St, Dublin
Purcell, Michael (Pte)	05/08/22	Tralee	Abbey St, Tralee
Sheehan, Pat (Pte)	26/08/22	N.A.	Co. Kerry

2. NATIONAL ARMY ACCIDENTAL DEATHS

Name	Date of Death	Place	Birth Place
Beatty, John (Pte)	23/08/22	Basin, Tralee	Lettermore, Galway
Looney, J. (Pte)	24/09/22	Killorglin barracks	Ballybrack, Kerry
McGrath, Matt (Capt)	23/09/22	Listowel	Feakle, Clare
McMahon, Tim (Lt)	25/08/22	Moyderwell	Miltown Malbay, Clare
Roche, Michael (Sgt)	25/08/22	Ballymullen barracks	Connolly, Clare
Woods, Denis (Pte)	23/08/22	Basin, Tralee	Mountshannon, Clare

3. NATIONAL ARMY FATALITIES

City/County of Origin	August 1922	September 1922
Belfast	1	1
Clare	3	1
Cork	1	–
Dublin	11	2
Galway	3	1
Kerry	3	6
Louth	–	1
Other	–	1

4. REPUBLICAN ARMY KILLED OR DIED OF WOUNDS

Name	Date of Death	Place	Birth Place
Drummond, Tom	24/08/22	Ballymullen barracks	Rae St, Tralee
Flynn, Thomas	02/08/22	Fenit	Spa, Tralee
Galvin, John	29/08/22	Ballyseedy wood	Killorglin, Kerry
Looney, Con	27/09/22	Killorglin	Kenmare, Kerry
Moriarty, Seán	27/08/22	Tralee	Walpole lane, Tralee
Murphy, Bertie	27/09/22	Killarney	Farranfore
Murphy, Patrick	27/09/22	Killorglin	Dooks, Glenbeigh
O'Sullivan, John	02/08/22	Spa, Tralee	Castlegregory
Ryle, Michael	05/08/22	Ballyseedy	Ballymacelligott

5. LOCATION OF DEATHS IN COMBAT DURING SUMMER CAMPAIGN IN KERRY

Location	National Army		Republican Army	
	August	September	August	September
Tralee	10	1	2	—
Ballyseedy	1	—	1	1
Fenit	—	—	1	—
Kilfenora	1	—	—	—
Spa	2	—	1	—
Castleisland	2	1	—	—
Castlemaine	1	—	—	—
Farranfore	—	2	—	—
Kilcummin	1	—	—	—
Killarney	2	—	—	1

Rathmore	—	1	—	—
Listowel	1	—	—	—
Killorglin	—	2	—	2
Kenmare	—	2	—	—
Cahirciveen	—	2	—	—
Other	1	2	—	—
TOTAL	22	13	5	4

6. COMPARATIVE STATISTICS, KERRY–DUBLIN, AUGUST–OCTOBER 1922

Casualties in street ambushes in Dublin

Month	National Army	Irregulars	Civilians	Total No. attacks
	Killed/ Wounded	Killed/ Wounded	Killed/ Wounded	
August	1/2	0/4	1/18	32
September	2/6	0/1	1/11	28
October	0/4	0/1	0/14	19

Casualties in the war in Kerry

August	22/c.50	5/n.a.	1/5	28
September	13/c.50	4/n.a.	2/2	19
October	8/5	n.a.	0/0	12

Sources for fatalities:

National Army: *Army Bulletin* and contemporary newspaper reports; *Who's Who in the Irish War of Independence and Civil War,* Padraig O'Farrell; *Kerry Landing*, Niall C.Harrington.

Republican army: All of the above. Also *The Last Post*, National Graves Association; *Tragedies of Kerry*, Dorothy Macardle; local history, various Kerry parishes.

General W.R.E. Murphy's memoir for his tenure as O/C Kerry Command (2 August 1922–2 January 1923) gives the following statistics for the period under his command: Free State army – 52 killed, 119 wounded; IRA – 79 killed, 119 wounded.

Endnotes

Chapter 1

1 Harrington, *Kerry Landing*, p. 89.

2 *Kerry People*, 18 February 1922.

3 Harrington, *Kerry Landing*, p. 10.

4 Gaughan, *Listowel and its Vicinity*, pp. 404–405.

5 *Kerry People*, 8 July 1922.

6 Murray, *Oracles of God*, pp. 151–152.

7 *Cork Examiner*, 3 July 1922.

8 *Cork Examiner*, 14 July 1922.

9 *Kerry People*, 29 July 1922.

10 Gaughan, *Listowel and its Vicinity*, p. 415.

11 *Cork Examiner*, 26 July 1922.

Chapter 2

1 Younger, *Ireland's Civil War*, p. 399.

2 *The Irish Times*, 13 September 1922, interview with Eoin O'Duffy.

3 Hopkinson, *The Irish War of Independence*, p. 125.

4 Younger, *Ireland's Civil War*, p. 314.

5 Harrington, *Kerry Landing*, pp. 74–75.

6 *Ibid.*, pp. 93–94.

7 *Cork Examiner*, 5 August 1922.

8 Dwyer, *Tans, Terror and Troubles*, p. 355.

9 Harrington, *Kerry Landing*, p. 104.

10 *Cork Examiner*, 7 August 1922.

11 *The Irish Times*, 9 August 1922.

12 Neeson, *The Irish Civil War 1922–23*, p. 97.

13 Younger, *Ireland's Civil War*, p. 398.

14 *The Irish Times*, 9 August 1922.

15 Ó Broin, *In Great Haste*, p. 216.

16 Mullins, *Memoir*, p. 61.

17 *Cork Examiner*, 12 August 1922.

18 *The Irish Times*, 12 August 1922.

19 Dwyer, *Tans, Terrors and Troubles*, pp. 369–372; Younger, *Ireland's Civil War*, p. 448; Duggan, *A History of the Irish Army*, p. 95.

20 Fitzgerald, *History of Ballymacelligott and its People*, p. 104.

21 Valiulis, *Portrait of a Revolutionary*, pp. 190–191.

22 Linge, 'The British navy and the Irish Civil War', pp. 60–71.

23 O'Shea, *The Ohermong Ambush*.

24 Hopkinson, *Green against Green*, p. 43.

25 Younger, *Ireland's Civil War*, p. 415.

26 *The Irish Times*, 25 August 1922.

27 *Cork Examiner*, 15 August 1922.

28 Mullins, *Memoirs*, p. 146.

29 *The Irish Times*, 15 August 1922.

30 *Kerry People*, 26 August 1922.

Chapter 3

1 *The Irish Times*, 14 August 1922.

2 *Freeman's Journal*, 30 August 1922.

3 *Ibid.*

4 Ó Ruairc, *Blood on the Banner*, pp. 162–167, provides details on Donal Lehane's involvement in the Rineen ambush, Miltown Malbay, Co. Clare, in September 1920 and the reprisals carried out on the Lehane family by crown forces.

5   O'Shea, *The Ohermong ambush*.

6   *Freeman's Journal*, August 1922.

7   *Cork Examiner*, 15 August 1922.

8   *Ibid.*, 16 August 1922.

9   *Ibid.*, 4 February 1922.

10 *Freeman's Journal*, 30 September 1922.

11 O'Malley & Dolan, *No Surrender Here*, p. 105.

12 Valiulis, *Almost a Rebellion* p. 37. Liam Tobin gives the composition of the Civil War Free State army as 50 per cent ex-British army, 40 per cent 'old' IRA and 10 per cent civilian.

13 *Cork Examiner*, 21 August 1922.

14 *Ibid.*, 23 August 1922.

15 Murphy, *When Youth was Mine*, pp. 201–202.

16 *Ibid.*

17 *Freeman's Journal*, 21 August 1922. Besides Colonel McGuinness, the other wounded were listed as Augustine McDonnell, Henry Taggart and Michael Kelly.

18 *Ibid.*

19 Harrington, *Kerry Landing*, p. 104.

20 *Ibid.*, p. 132.

21 *Cork Examiner*, 22 August 1922.

22 *Freeman's Journal*, 26 August 1922.

23 *Cork Examiner*, 23 & 25 August 1922. The *Cork Examiner* gives the number of republicans under escort as 105 prisoners, whereas the *Kerry People* newspaper lists the number as eleven.

24 *Freeman's Journal*, 25 August 1922.

25 *Cork Examiner*, 28 August 1922.

26 *The Irish Times*, 24 August 1922. Patrick was a brother of the late Dan Allman, who lost his life at the Headford Junction ambush in March 1921.

27 Mullins, *Memoir*, pp. 149–150.

28 *Freeman's Journal*, 25 August 1922.

29 *Cork Examiner*, 30 August 1922.

30 Harrington, *Kerry Landing*, p. 138.

31 *Cork Examiner*, 28 August 1922.

32 *The Irish Times*, 16 December 1922.

33 Mullins, *Memoir*, pp. 151–153.

34 Account based on reports in the *Freeman's Journal*, 30 August 1922, and *The Irish Times*, 30 August 1922.

35 *Cork Examiner*, 28 August 1922.

36 *Freeman's Journal*, 30 August 1922.

37 *Cork Examiner*, 7 September 1922.

38 Murphy, *General W.R.E. Murphy and the Irish Civil War 1922–1923*.

Chapter 4

1 *Cork Examiner*, 4 September 1922.

2 MacEoin, *Survivors*, p. 359.

3 *Freeman's Journal*, 8 September 1922.

4 *Cork Examiner*, 21 September 1922.

5 *Ibid.*, 8 September 1922.

6 *Ibid.*

7 Regan, *The Irish Counter Revolution, 1921–1936*, p. 107.

8 O'Shea, *Ohermong Ambush*, pp. 3–4.

9 O'Malley & Dolan, *No Surrender Here*, p. 159.

10 *Ibid.*, p. 159.

11 *Freeman's Journal*, 14 September 1922.

12 Murphy, *When Youth Was Mine*, pp. 205–208.

13 *The Irish Times*, 14 September 1922.

14 Younger, *Ireland's Civil War*, p. 450.

15 MacEoin, *The IRA in the Twilight Years*, p. 619.

16 *Freeman's Journal*, 14 September 1922.

17 *The Irish Times*, 14 September 1922.

18 Younger, *Ireland's Civil War*, pp. 451–452.

19 Murphy, *When Youth was Mine*, pp. 205–208.

20 *The Irish Times*, 14 September 1922.

21 Hopkinson, *Green against Green*, p. 207.

22 *Freeman's Journal*, 14 September 1922.

23 *The Irish Times*, 14 September 1922.

24 Reminiscences of my mother, Anne Doyle (Houlihan). Family folklore of her uncle Barth Houlihan's visit to Kenmare shortly after the fall of the town (9 September attack) to republicans.

25 *The Irish Times*, 14 September 1922.

26 Hopkinson, *Green against Green*, pp. 206–207.

27 Younger, *Ireland's Civil War*, p. 451.

28 Murphy, *When Youth was Mine*, pp. 210–211.

29 *Cork Examiner*, 23 September 1922.

30 *Freeman's Journal*, 15 September 1922.

31 *Ibid*, 18 September 1922.

32 *Ibid*.

33 Turvey, 'Politics, War and Revolution in Kenmare district, 1916–1923', pp. 99–125.

34 O'Malley & Dolan, *No Surrender Here*, p. 180.

35 Lynch, *Tarbert: An Unfinished Biography*, pp. 400–402.

36 *Ibid*.

37 *Ibid*.

38 *Freeman's Journal*, 15 September 1922.

39 *Cork Examiner*, 30 September 1922.

40 *Freeman's Journal*, 27 September 1922.

41 *Cork Examiner*, 30 September 1922.

Chapter 5

1   Murphy, *General W.R.E. Murphy and the Irish Civil War*, p. 20.

2   *Ibid.*, p. 6.

3   *Cork Examiner*, 13 September 1922.

4   Valiulis, *Portrait of a Revolutionary*, p. 188.

5   *The Irish Times*, 23 September 1922.

6   *Cork Examiner*, 22 September 1922.

7   Murphy, *General W.R.E. Murphy and the Irish Civil War*, p. 25.

8   *Ibid.*

9   *Ibid.*

10 *Freeman's Journal*, 23 September 1922.

11 Murphy, *General W.R.E. Murphy and the Irish Civil War*, p. 23.

12 *Cork Examiner*, 26 September 1922.

13 *The Irish Times*, 23 September 1922.

14 *Freeman's Journal*, 27 September 1922.

15 *The Irish Times*, 29 September 1922.

16 *Freeman's Journal*, 27 September 1922.

17 Murphy, *General W.R.E. Murphy and the Irish Civil War*, p. 28.

18 *Freeman's Journal*, 4 October 1922.

19 *Cork Examiner*, 6 October 1922.

20 Short account of 27 September 1922 assault on Killorglin by Maurice 'Mossie' Roche in the author's possession.

21 *Cork Examiner*, 6 October 1922.

22 Roche, document cited above.

23 Austin Reilly, Killorglin. Conversation on his mother Mary's (née O'Sullivan) involvement in Cumann na mBan, Killorglin, during the assault on Killorglin in September 1922.

24 *Cork Examiner*, 6 October 1922.

25 *Ibid.*

26 *Freeman's Journal*, 4 October 1922.

27 Murphy, *General W.R.E. Murphy and the Irish Civil War*, p. 28. General Murphy refers to a Father O'Sullivan as the parish priest of Killorglin, but the parish priest was actually Father James Nolan.

28 *Cork Examiner*, 6 October 1922.

29 Regan, *The Irish Counter Revolution, 1922–1936*, p. 108. A letter from David Robinson to Gavan Duffy.

30 *Freeman's Journal*, 4 October 1922.

31 Murphy, *General W.R.E. Murphy and the Irish Civil War*, p. 28.

32 *Ibid.*, p. 31.

33 *Ibid.*, p. 30.

34 *Freeman's Journal*, 6 October 1922.

35 *Ibid.*, 3 October 1922.

36 Murphy, *General W.R.E. Murphy and the Irish Civil War*, p. 37.

37 *Ibid.*, p. 39.

38 *Ibid.*, p. 41.

Chapter 6

1 Harrington, *Kerry Landing*, p. 167.

2 Ryan, *The Real Chief*, p. 136.

3 O'Farrell, *Who's Who in the Irish War of Independence and the Civil War*, abstracts of details pp. 102–120.

4 *Ibid.*

5 *The Irish Times*, 11 October 1922.

6 *Cork Examiner*, 29 September 1922.

Select Bibliography

Abbott, Richard, *Police Casualties in Ireland, 1919-1922* (Mercier Press, Cork 2000)

Brennan, Michael, *The War in Clare 1911-1921* (Four Courts Press, Dublin 1980)

Coogan, T.P., *Michael Collins* (Hutchinson, London 1990)

Dolan, Anne, *Commemorating the Civil War, 1923–2000* (Cambridge University Press, 2003)

Duggan, John P., *A History of the Irish Army* (Gill and Macmillan, Dublin 1998)

Dwyer, T. Ryle, *Michael Collins and the Treaty* (Mercier Press, Cork 1981)

Dwyer, T. Ryle, *Tans, Terror and Troubles: Kerry's real fighting story, 1913-1923* (Mercier Press, Cork 2001)

Dwyer, T. Ryle, *The Squad* (Mercier Press, Cork 2005)

Fitzgerald, Bobby (ed.), *History of Ballymacelligott and its People* (Ballymacelligott Active Retirement Asssociation, 1997)

Garvin, Tom, 1922, *The Birth of Irish Democracy* (Gill and Macmillan, Dublin 1996

Gaughan, J. Anthony, *Listowel and its Vicinity* (Mercier Press, Cork 1973)

Griffith, Kenneth, *Curious Journey* (Mercier Press, Cork 1998)

Harrington, Niall C., *Kerry Landing, August 1922* (Anvil Books, Dublin 1992)

Hopkinson, Michael, *Green against Green* (Gill and Macmillan, Dublin 1998)

Hopkinson, Michael, *The Irish War of Independence* (Gill and Macmillan, Dublin 2002)

Joy, Sinead, *The IRA in Kerry, 1916–1921* (Collins Press, Cork 2005)

Kissane, Bill, *The Politics of the Irish Civil War* (Oxford University Press, Oxford 2005)

Laffan, Michael, *The Resurrection of Ireland, The Sinn Féin Party 1916–1923* (Cambridge University Press, Cambridge 1999)

Linge, John, 'The British navy and the Irish Civil War', *Irish Historical Studies*, Vol. XXXI, No. 121, May 1998

Lynch, Patrick J., *Tarbert: An Unfinished Biography* (Shanagolden, Limerick 2008)

Macardle, Dorothy, *Tragedies of Kerry* (Irish Freedom Press, Dublin 1988)

McEoin, Uinseann, *Survivors* (Argenta Publications, Dublin 1980)

McEoin, Uinseann, *The IRA in the Twilight Years* (Argenta Publications, Dublin 1997(

McGarry, Fearghal, *Eoin O'Duffy: A Self-Made Hero* (Oxford University Press, Oxford 2005)

McMahon, Paul, *British Spies and Irish Rebels: British intelligence and Ireland 1916–1945* (Boydell Press, 2008)

Mullins, Billy, *Memoir* (Kenno Press, Tralee 1983)

Murphy, Jeremiah, *When Youth was Mine: a memoir of Kerry, 1902–1925* (Mentor Press, Dublin 1998)

Murphy, Karl, *General W.R.E. Murphy and the Irish Civil War 1922–1923*, unpublished MA Thesis, NUI, Maynooth 1994

Murray, Patrick, *Oracles of God: The Catholic Church and Irish politics 1922–1937* (UCD Press, Dublin 2000)

Neeson, Eoin, *The Civil War in Ireland* (Mercier Press, Cork 1966)

Ó Broin, Leon, *In Great Haste* (Gill and Macmillan, Dublin 1988)

O'Farrell, Padraig, *Who's Who in the Irish War of Independence and Civil War* (Lilliput Press, Dublin 1996)

O'Malley, Cormac K.H. & Dolan, Anne, *No Surrender Here: the Civil War Papers of Ernie O'Malley, 1922–1924* (Lilliput Press, Dublin 2007)

Ó Ruairc, Padraig Óg, *Blood on the Banner: the Republican Struggle in Clare 1916-1923* (Mercier Press, Cork 2009)

O'Shea, Michael Christopher, *The Ohermong Ambush* (Cahirciveen, 2003)

Regan, John M., *The Irish Counter Revolution, 1921–1936* (Gill and Macmillan, Dublin 1991)

Ryan, Meda, *The Real Chief: the Story of Liam Lynch* (Mercier Press, Cork 1986)

Townshend, Charles, *Ireland: the 20th Century* (Arnold, London 1999)

Turvey, Claire, 'Politics, War and Revolution in Kenmare district, 1916–1923', in *Kerry History and Archaeology Society Journal*, Vol. 6, 2006, pp. 99–125

Valiulis, Maryann G., *Almost a Rebellion: the Irish Army Mutiny of 1924* (Tower Books, Cork 1985)

Valiulis, Maryann G., *Portrait of a Revolutionary: General Richard Mulcahy and the foundation of the Irish Free State* (Irish Academic Press, Dublin 1992)

Younger, Calton, *Ireland's Civil War* (Fontana Books, London 1968)

Walker, Brian M., *Election Results, 1922–1992* (Royal Irish Academy, Dublin 1992)

INDEX